The American Dream Delayed:
The Harada Family's Quest for
Civil Rights

Funded by a
Library Services & Technology Act (LSTA) grant

Riverside Public Library

THE INTERNMENT OF JAPANESE AMERICANS DURING WORLD WAR II

MILESTONES
IN
AMERICAN HISTORY

THE INTERNMENT OF JAPANESE AMERICANS DURING WORLD WAR II

DETENTION OF AMERICAN CITIZENS

JOHN C. DAVENPORT

CHELSEA HOUSE
PUBLISHERS
An imprint of Infobase Publishing

Chelsea House
An imprint of Infobase Publishing
132 West 31st Street
New York, NY 10001

Library of Congress Cataloging-in-Publication Data

Davenport, John, 1960-
The internment of Japanese Americans during World War II : detention of American citizens / John Davenport.
    p. cm. — (Milestones in American history)
Includes bibliographical references and index.
ISBN 978-1-60413-681-4 (hardcover)
1. Japanese Americans—Evacuation and relocation, 1942-1945—Juvenile literature.
2. World War, 1939–1945—Japanese Americans—Juvenile literature. 3. World War, 1939–1945—Prisoners and prisons, American—Juvenile literature. I. Title. II. Series.

D769.8.A6D378 2010
940.53'1773—dc22   2009029613

Chelsea House books are available at special discounts when purchased in bulk quantities for businesses, associations, institutions, or sales promotions. Please call our Special Sales Department in New York at (212) 967-8800 or (800) 322-8755.

You can find Chelsea House on the World Wide Web at http://www.chelseahouse.com

Text design by Erik Lindstrom
Cover design by Alicia Post
Composition by Keith Trego
Cover printed by Yurchak Printing, Landisville, Pa.
Book printed and bound by Yurchak Printing, Landisville, Pa.

Printed in the United States of America

This book is printed on acid-free paper.

All links and Web addresses were checked and verified to be correct at the time of publication. Because of the dynamic nature of the Web, some addresses and links may have changed since publication and may no longer be valid.

CONTENTS

Day of Infamy

The news from Hawaii shattered the calm December Sunday across the United States. Radios from coast to coast delivered the word that America was at war: "We are interrupting this program for a special report. At this very moment, Japanese airplanes are attacking the United States Naval Base at Pearl Harbor on the island of Oahu in the Hawaiian Islands. Stay tuned to this program for further developments."[1] Americans stared at one another in stunned disbelief. Everyone knew that diplomatic relations with Japan had been deteriorating for months, ever since the United States had cut off oil shipments to the island empire in July 1941 in response to the Japanese occupation of French Indochina. Matters only grew worse with the government's decision that same summer to freeze Japanese assets in American banks. No one expected war, though, at least not one that would begin with a brazen attack on America's main Pacific naval base.

In cities and towns across the country, therefore, the news of the raid on Pearl Harbor produced shock and then rage. "Have you heard the news?" a Connecticut college student yelled at his roommates on December 7, using the racial slur common for the time. "Japs have bombed Pearl Harbor. . . . We're now at war."[2] Within hours of the attack, Americans were caught in the vise-like grip of "Pearl Harbor panic."[3] Wild rumors swirled about—the Japanese were bombing California; a Japanese task force was preparing to invade the United States; Japanese spies in Washington State were relaying military information via flashlight to enemy submarines off the West Coast. Fear, misinformation, and confusion soon led to paranoia. The enemy was everywhere, it seemed. As Americans came to accept the reality of war with Japan, they began to search among themselves for spies and traitors. Their jittery gaze quickly fell upon Japanese Americans.

In Hawaii, where 38 percent of the population was of Japanese ancestry, the attack on Pearl Harbor generated similar fears to those felt on the mainland. Those fears, though, were mixed with a sense of shame and apprehension on the part of some Japanese Americans. "I felt bad," one man recalled, "because to think our mother country had attacked my country."[4] Others knew that their white neighbors might indirectly blame them for the actions of their ethnic relatives in Japan, but they reasoned that a shared sense of unity at a time of national emergency would bind together all Americans, regardless of race. Japanese Americans who held such hopes were soon disabused of the notion that patriotism trumped race in mid-twentieth-century America. The bombs had scarcely stopped falling at Pearl Harbor before the insults began to rain down on Japanese Americans. "You Jap SOB," a pair of white women screamed at a man strolling down a street in Hawaii. "I'm an American!" he shouted back.[5]

On the morning of December 7, 1941, the Japanese navy made a surprise attack against the U.S. naval base at Pearl Harbor, Hawaii. U.S. losses and casualties were massive, including 2,402 persons killed and 1,282 wounded. Above are three stricken U.S. battleships: *(left to right)* USS *West Virginia*, which was severely damaged; USS *Tennessee*, which was damaged; and USS *Arizona*, which was sunk.

FEAR AND SUSPICION

Japanese Americans living in Hawaii and along the West Coast of the United States could feel the popular resentment rising against them on December 7. Neighbors who had shared their lives with them for years suddenly refused to look at their Japanese-American friends. A young girl remembered how, before the attack on Pearl Harbor, merchants and others she passed on her way to school greeted her warmly. Afterward, however, the mood on the streets suddenly changed. "There goes that little Jap!" the girl recalled hearing. "I'm looking around. Who's a Jap? Who's a Jap? Then it dawned on me, I'm the Jap."[6] Cold stares and whispered warnings about infiltrators and spies soon became commonplace. Coworkers who had been close associates only days earlier now scrutinized Japanese Americans on the job as if examining an alien presence. Frustrated, like the adults around her, by the implicit connection with the Imperial Navy pilots who had caused the deaths of more than 2,000 Americans on Oahu, a little Japanese-American girl asked her mother, "How can they say we're the ones who did this? We don't have any planes or bombs!"[7] Even though more than half of the civilians killed during the Japanese raid were Japanese Americans, latent racial hatred sprang to life in the aftermath of the day that President Franklin Delano Roosevelt, in his speech to Congress requesting a declaration of war, said would "live in infamy."[8]

For the average non-Japanese American, all Japanese living in the United States, either alien (noncitizen) or citizen, shared in the guilt assigned to the Pearl Harbor attackers. All were viewed as real or potential enemies. The government, however, had only enemy aliens in mind when, on the evening of December 8, it ordered the "summary apprehension" of any Japanese noncitizen "deemed dangerous to the public peace or safety of the United States."[9] Almost immediately, alien Japanese residents were rounded up and jailed on the West Coast and Hawaii. By December 11, 1,370 foreign Japanese were being held in detention; two months later, that number would reach 2,192 Japanese in the western states, with another 879 in Hawaii.

Possible arrest and certain hostility awaited anyone who so much as looked as if they were Japanese. (Chinese Americans, given that China was now a U.S. ally, were protected by being accorded the status of "honorary Caucasians."[10]) No one, however, had yet suggested any kind of mass arrest of Japanese Americans. Racial violence was similarly out of the question. The *Los Angeles Times*, for example, in an editorial on December 8, went to great lengths to remind its readers that "thousands of Japanese here and in other coast cities [are] good Americans, born and educated as such."[11] The newspaper added an appeal for calm and urged that there be "no riots, no mob law."[12] The *Sacramento Bee* went as far as to equate anti-Japanese sentiment with Nazism. "Racial hatred belongs in the arsenal of Nazi weapons," a *Bee* editorial argued. "The wise and sensible American will avoid [racism] as he would a deadly poison or fatal pestilence [and respect] the traditional and time-honored American policy—fairness to all who love the Flag, no matter where the accident of parentage may have located their birthplace."[13]

AN IDEA IS BORN

Appeals for restraint, such as those in the *Los Angeles Times* and *Sacramento Bee*, came from many quarters. Most Americans responded positively by withholding any final judgment on their Japanese-American countrymen, at least for the time being. Initially, then, the detention of Japanese aliens—and Italian and German noncitizens after Germany and Italy declared war on the United States on December 11—satisfied public demands for internal security. It seemed reasonable to most people that detaining aliens from Axis countries (those countries at war with the United States during World War II) was a necessary step in protecting the nation from potential spies and saboteurs. It also appeared logical that doing so effectively neutralized the danger.

Yet as the days and weeks passed, a growing chorus of voices called for stronger action, especially with regard to Japanese living on the West Coast. A sizable number of these residents were Issei, men and women born in Japan and thus precluded

After the attack on Pearl Harbor, anti-Japanese sentiment reached its peak. The loyalty and trustworthiness of all Asians were questioned, including Chinese Americans, who faced their own racial prejudices. Here, Joe Chiang, Washington correspondent for the *Chinese Nationalist Daily*, wears a handwritten badge that reads, "Chinese reporter, NOT Japanese, please," as he shows his press card to a guard at the gate to the White House press room.

from ever becoming American citizens, and some were Kibei, young U.S.-born Japanese sent to study in Japan. The majority, however, were Nisei, native-born American citizens with few or no connections to the parent country, who nonetheless were indistinguishable ethnically from the other groups. Because Issei, Nisei, and Kibei seemed so closely linked in the eyes of non-Japanese Americans, questions began to arise concerning the loyalty and trustworthiness of all three groups. Out of ignorance and confusion, webs of suspicion were soon spun around the entire Japanese-American community. Blatant racism would quickly harden those webs into barbed-wire fences surrounding internment camps.

By late January 1942, respected politicians, military officers, newspaper editors, and average Americans alike were thinking in terms of a broader threat to wartime security and a more general response. Simple detention of enemy aliens posing an obvious risk was no longer enough to calm the fears of a nation traumatized by a surprise attack on its territory and the subsequent thrust into the Second World War. Calls echoed from one corner of the country to another demanding harsher government measures to deal with any possible danger emanating from anyone who shared an ancestry with the country's new enemies. This applied in particular to the Japanese—Asians who traditionally had been viewed as racial and ethnic outsiders. As the United States prepared for a long and brutal struggle against the empire of Japan, Americans in ever greater numbers began to talk about a mass evacuation of Japanese Americans from areas deemed to be likely targets of another Pearl Harbor-like attack. The public was speaking, and in Washington, D.C., the president was listening.

The Japanese in America

The leading edge of what became a wave of Asian immigration to the United States rolled across the Pacific from China in the mid-nineteenth century. Pushed by poverty at home and pulled by the discovery of gold in California in 1848, Chinese men left the towns and villages of their birth for a land they knew as *Gam Saan*, "Gold Mountain."[1] There, they hoped to find riches and a brighter future, as did so many other gold seekers, along the banks of the American River. Instead, Chinese immigrants were met with resentment on the part of white Californians that quickly evolved into fierce racial hatred. Despite their willingness to share equally in the backbreaking labor of the Gold Rush, the Chinese were marginalized, discriminated against, and routinely driven from the gold fields. Acts of violence directed against Chinese miners became commonplace.

By the mid-1860s, the almost exclusively male Chinese community in the western United States was confined to racially segregated Chinatowns, the largest of which was in the port city of San Francisco. For gainful employment, the residents of San Francisco's Chinese enclave could aspire to a narrow range of menial or service jobs, most frequently shopkeeping, laundering, construction work, or gang labor on the Central Pacific Railroad, which was blasting through the Sierra Nevada mountains in an effort to create a rail link to the cities of the Midwest and ultimately the East Coast. And yet, despite segregation, racial animosity, and severely limited job opportunities, the Chinese established themselves as a fixture in the social life of the American West and an integral component of the region's economy. Chinese immigrants had started to become Chinese Americans and, in the process, had opened a door to the United States that other Asian groups would soon pass through.

THE JAPANESE FOLLOW

As it became clear that the Chinese presence in America represented a permanent alteration in the West's demographics, white hostility grew more intense. White workers, who had only recently begun to organize themselves in the face of industrial capitalism, feared that Chinese competition in the labor market would decrease their wages and ruin their efforts to build unions. The Chinese were also viewed as crude and barbaric in their customs. The same, at least in the beginning, was not said about the second wave of Asian immigrants, who came from Japan. The West's preeminent newspaper, the *San Francisco Chronicle*, in fact, stated flatly in 1869 that "the objections raised against the Chinese ... cannot be alleged against the Japanese." Unlike the immigrants from China, the newspaper concluded, those from Japan were "gentlemen of refinement and culture."[2]

Popular animosity increasingly turned toward the Japanese, however, as their numbers in America increased. When, in

1882, Congress passed the Chinese Exclusion Act, effectively choking off any further Chinese immigration, anti-Asian sentiment was redirected and targeted against the only remaining large Asian community. Japanese immigrants had been coming to the United States in growing numbers because of the economic chaos and political turmoil that followed the restoration of the Meiji emperor. Hobbled by the collapse of its agricultural sector, Japan's economy slipped into a deep recession in the 1880s. The island nation's farm families were struck hard by declining agricultural prices as well as soaring imperial taxes. "The distress among the agricultural classes," the *Japan Weekly Mail* editorialized in 1884, "has reached a point never before attained."[3] Farmers in many parts of Japan faced imminent poverty and hunger; emigration, at least for the young, offered the only real hope for recovery.

Young Japanese men begged to be allowed to leave their ancestral homes. "By all means," they implored their elders, "let me go to America."[4] Their fathers soon relented, allowing their adult sons to emigrate, with the mainland United States or the then-independent Hawaii as their destinations. They were welcomed in Hawaii by sugarcane plantation owners desperate for laborers to work the cane fields and on the mainland by farmers seeking inexpensive hands to cultivate the rapidly expanding acres of farmland on the West Coast, especially in California's Central Valley. As early as 1890, no fewer than 30,000 Japanese men—and women, if the immigrants came as a family—had arrived in Hawaii, and more than 2,000 had made their way to the western United States.

THE WHITE REACTION

The Japanese who came to America in the late nineteenth century experienced the full force of the racism that had been previously reserved for the Chinese. The 1870s and 1880s had seen an extended spasm of anti-Chinese violence. San Francisco, in particular, endured a series of anti-Chinese riots in

Denis Kearney, an Irish immigrant, gained popularity among the working class in San Francisco by protesting against immigrant Chinese workers. As secretary of the Workingman's Party of California, he criticized the Central Pacific Railroad, who employed the immigrants in large numbers, and often led violent attacks (depicted above) on the Chinese.

1877 that resulted in the burning of parts of Chinatown and random physical assaults aimed at any available Chinese target. Led by the rabble-rousing labor leader Denis Kearney, workers rampaged through the city's streets. The 1882 Chinese Exclusion Act was a response, in part, to Kearney's reign of terror

in San Francisco, but its passage denied him and his follow-
ers fresh victims for future racist attacks. In this instance, the
recently arrived Japanese served as the new focal point for the
hatred and abuse meted out by Kearney and others like him.
Few men could match Kearney in spitting rhetorical venom at
Japanese immigrants. Deriding them as just "another breed of
Asiatic slaves [imported] to fill up the gap made vacant by the
Chinese," Kearney demanded an immediate end to Japanese
immigration and the perceived Japanese threat to white workers' jobs.[5] San Francisco's mayor, James D. Phelan, claimed
to "have nothing against the Japanese," but even this career
politician agreed that "as they will not assimilate with us . . .
let them keep a respectful distance."[6]

Spared the worst of the overheated rhetoric that characterized the white reaction to Japanese immigration on the
mainland, Hawaii nevertheless suffered its share of racial
anxiety over its increasingly large Japanese presence. White
Hawaiians, however, had neither the luxury nor the willingness to limit the number of Japanese coming in search of a
living. Hawaiian planters sorely needed Japanese labor and
could not afford to heed mainland-type calls for exclusion.
Rather, they sought to encourage Japanese immigration while
simultaneously diluting Japanese influence in Hawaiian society by importing large numbers of workers from Korea and
the Philippines. They hoped that these groups, augmented
by a growing Portuguese managerial class, would help nul-
lify, or invalidate, any power gained by the Japanese as their
population rose. A minority of planters schemed not only
to reduce Japanese influence but also the numbers of the
Japanese community itself. As one planter argued in 1903,
"Get a large number of Koreans in the country . . . and drive
the [Japanese] out."[7]

Scattered propositions such as these came to nothing in
the end. Far from leaving Hawaii, Japanese continued to arrive
there and on the mainland in ever greater numbers. In 1900,

for example, 2 percent of the population of California claimed Japanese ancestry. Japanese farmers, at that time, owned and operated only 29 farms, comprising a mere 4,698 acres (1,901 hectares) of the state's arable land. Yet, by 1910, the amount of soil farmed by Japanese had ballooned to 194,742 acres (78,809 ha). The success of immigrant farmers in California was so sudden and startling that white agricultural interests demanded a halt to any further land purchases by Japanese and, ultimately, an end to immigration from Japan along the lines of the Chinese Exclusion Act. Indeed, some nativist groups called for the consolidation of Japanese and Chinese into a single category of unwanted foreigners. In May 1905, they came together as the Oriental Exclusion League.

San Franciscans, already troubled by the vibrant Chinese community in their midst, were among some of the first Californians to enact policies designed to lump Japanese and Chinese together into one undifferentiated Asian mass. The first of these policies involved the city's public schools. Determined to enforce more fully the separation of Asians and whites, the San Francisco school board voted in October 1906 to place Japanese students in Chinese schools. Unaware of the ethnic hostility that the Japanese felt toward the Chinese, the school board inadvertently touched off an international crisis. Sensitive to the slightest hint of racial insult, the Japanese government vigorously protested the board's decision directly to the U.S. president, Theodore Roosevelt. Japanese officials implied that the discrimination in San Francisco could lead to a severing of diplomatic relations, or worse. Rumors mentioned war as a possible result of the school decision. Roosevelt himself worried that "the mob of a single city [might] plunge us into war."[8] He thus responded to the Japanese protests by ordering the school board to rescind its policy. In exchange, the Japanese agreed, in the so-called Gentlemen's Agreement of 1906, to strictly limit the number of immigrants leaving Japan for the United States.

THE GROWTH OF JAPANESE AMERICA

Roosevelt's compromise with the Japanese government not only avoided a diplomatic showdown, perhaps even a war, but it also helped unite those Japanese immigrants who had established themselves in America. In Hawaii, Japanese cane workers organized a union and struck for better wages and working conditions in 1909. Japanese farmers in California, meanwhile, continued to prosper. True, by 1912, most Americans continued to agree with men like President Woodrow Wilson, who argued that the Japanese "do not blend with the Caucasian race,"[9] still others had to admit, as the *San Francisco Chronicle* did, that the newcomers possessed "pluck and intelligence."[10]

Pluck and intelligence were needed in abundance as Japanese immigrants strove to become successful Americans. Even with a 1913 California law that prohibited further Japanese land purchases, Japanese-owned farms continued to thrive, sending to market, in total dollar value, 10 percent of California's agricultural output—at a time when Japanese held only 1 percent of the state's farmland. The California strawberry crop demonstrated how much Japanese farmers did with what little they had. In 1910, Japanese farms produced 70 percent of the strawberries grown in the state. All along California's great Central Valley, Japanese immigrants were hard at work turning the semiarid landscape into productive acreage. As one proudly proclaimed, "Japanese took that land, cleared it, and made it fine farming land."[11]

The Japanese population similarly flourished. From 1885 to 1924, more than 80,000 Japanese came to Hawaii and stayed. More than 60,000 lived on the mainland, of whom 27 percent were American-born Nisei, virtually indistinguishable from any other American except by their Asian characteristics. In California alone, 2 percent of the population was of Japanese ancestry, both Nisei and their older Japanese-born Issei relatives. So thoroughly and inextricably were the Japanese integrated into American life in the early decades of the twentieth century that most shared the sentiment of Asakichi Inouye, grandfather of the future U.S. senator Daniel Inouye. When asked about his adopted homeland, the elder Inouye responded simply, "My children are here . . . it is here that I have passed most of the days of my life. . . . [Japan] has become for us a strange place."[12]

FEAR, SURVEILLANCE, AND DISCRIMINATION

As the 1920s dawned, the Japanese were firmly and irreversibly entrenched in American life and society. Clearly, the Japanese were in America to stay, so those of a racist bent had to content themselves with trying to choke off any further immigration and with barring naturalization (the procedure by which the United States confers citizenship upon a foreign national) as a route to eventual citizenship. Journalist Cornelius Vanderbilt Jr., in 1921, spoke for a sizable minority of Americans when he wrote of a general fear that "we are drawing near unto the crossroads of America's future Oriental destiny. Japan's further penetration can mean nothing save a direct insult to us."[13] Vanderbilt went on to argue in favor of total exclusion of Japanese immigrants. A young Franklin Delano Roosevelt agreed with Vanderbilt's assessment from a genetic standpoint. The future president claimed that there was only one "true reason" to cut off further immigration from Japan, and that was the "undesirability of mixing the blood of the two peoples."[14]

Listening intently to these and similar calls for an end to Japanese immigration, the U.S. Supreme Court, in 1922, ruled that Japanese newcomers did not qualify for the naturalization process. Holding that only Europeans and Africans, as foreign relatives of the original non-native inhabitants of the American republic, could be naturalized under current law, the court dismissed the citizenship application of Takeo Ozawa, a 20-year resident of Hawaii. Writing for the majority, Justice George Sutherland concluded that, even though Ozawa "was a graduate of the Berkeley, California, High School, had been nearly three years a student at the University of California, had educated his children in American schools, his family had attended American churches, and he had maintained the use of the English language in his home [and] was well qualified by character and education for citizenship," he was "clearly of a race that is not Caucasian."[15] Ozawa was thus by accident of race ineligible to become an American citizen. Two years after the Supreme Court's ruling, Congress formally prohibited any further immigration from Japan with the Immigration Act of 1924.

From this point on, foreign-born individuals, who represented 48 percent of the Japanese population of America, were effectively disenfranchised in their adopted homeland. The remaining 52 percent, however, were already American citizens by birth. Nevertheless, both groups were increasingly viewed as potential threats, no longer to racial but to national security, as tensions between the United States and Japan grew during the 1920s and 1930s. Japan's occupation of Manchuria (a region in northeast China) in 1931 put the island empire on a collision course with the United States, as the two nations vied for control of the Pacific Ocean. Reasonable concerns over possible espionage soon gave way to paranoia as Americans began to imagine Japanese agents everywhere. Even the State Department fell prey to fears of enemy spies lurking in Japanese-American neighborhoods, fraternal lodges, and community centers. A departmental report in 1934 concluded that there were Japanese "agents in every large city in this country and on the West Coast. . . . When war breaks out, the entire Japanese population on the West Coast will rise and commit sabotage."[16] Two years later, President Franklin Roosevelt suggested that the security risk posed by Japanese in Hawaii was so great that anyone having contact with ships from Japan "should be secretly but definitely identified and his or her name placed on a special list of those who would be the first to be placed in a concentration camp in the event of trouble."[17] Routine surveillance of Japanese Americans by the Army G-2 intelligence

This 1938 cover from U.S. magazine *Ken* depicts a caricature of a Japanese spy. Before the attack on Pearl Harbor, Japanese Americans did everything possible to prove their loyalty. Still, the media often portrayed them negatively, leading to a public distrust of Asians.

branch, the Office of Naval Intelligence, and the Federal Bureau of Investigation began soon afterward.

Despite repeated Japanese-American statements of loyalty and assertions that at least American-born Nisei had burned "our bridges [to Japan] behind us,"[18] many officials worried over the supposed military threat represented by the Japanese community. Of even greater concern to the government were the thousands of Japanese foreign nationals living in the United States. By the late 1930s, American intelligence agencies had compiled a list of more than 2,000 Japanese aliens, known as the A-B-C list. Broken down into three categories, individuals were listed as being either A, "sinister enough to warrant top billing"; B, "potentially dangerous"; or C, "watched because of their pro-Japanese inclination."[19] While not officially included on the federal list, Japanese Americans were being closely

THE JAPANESE AMERICAN CITIZENS LEAGUE CREED

The premier Japanese-American civil-rights group in the early twentieth century was the Japanese American Citizens League. Founded in 1929, the JACL was dedicated to protecting the rights of all Japanese and demonstrating their loyalty to the United States. Such loyalty was expressed clearly and unequivocally in the JACL creed, an excerpt of which follows:

I am proud that I am an American citizen of Japanese ancestry, for my very background makes me appreciate more fully the wonderful advantages of this nation. I believe in her institutions, ideals, and traditions; I glory in her heritage; I boast of her history; I trust in her future. She has granted me liberties and opportunities such as no individual enjoys in the world today. She has given me an education befitting kings. She has entrusted me with the responsibilities of the franchise. She has permitted me to build a home, to earn a livelihood, to worship, think, speak, and act as I please— as a free man equal to every other man. Although some individu-

watched for any hint of sympathy for the ancestral homeland or its government.

As war with Japan evolved from being possible to likely being inevitable by 1941, talk of acts of sabotage and espionage by Japanese on the West Coast grew louder. Despite indisputable evidence that Japanese Americans were "pathetically eager"[20] to demonstrate their loyalty, a report to the president in the fall of 1941 warned, "There are still Japanese in the United States who will tie dynamite around their waist and make a human bomb out of themselves."[21] Even those who

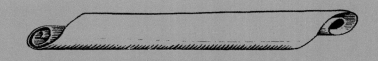

als may discriminate against me, I shall never become bitter or lose faith, for I know that such persons are not representative of the American people. . . . Because I believe in America, and I trust she believes in me, and because I have received innumerable benefits from her, I pledge myself to do honor to her at all times and all places; to support her constitution; to obey her laws; to respect her flag; to defend her against all enemies, foreign and domestic; to actively assume my duties and obligations as a citizen, cheerfully and without any reservations whatsoever, in the hope that I may become a better American in a greater America.*

Through the JACL, Japanese Americans pledged their loyalty to the very nation and government that would oversee their removal and internment in 1942.

---

* Roger Daniels, *Prisoners Without Trial: Japanese Americans in World War II*. New York: Hill and Wang, 1993, pp. 20–21.

harbored no such exaggerated fears of Japanese suicide bombers still wondered if Japanese Americans could be fully trusted if the United States went to war with Japan.

In the summer of 1941, the FBI broke up a Japanese spy ring, led by an undercover Japanese Imperial Navy officer and composed of foreign-born Japanese and Nisei. Never really a credible threat to American security, the ring was nonetheless part of an official Japanese military espionage project that incorporated Japanese Americans. Troubled by the mere notion of a hidden Asian enemy in their midst, many Americans saw the spy ring as an indication that their Japanese neighbors, at the very least, might be of dubious loyalty and, at worst, might be in league with the empire of Japan. The situation was primed for hysteria and tragedy.

Executive
Order 9066

The news of the Japanese attack on Pearl Harbor was only a few hours old when President Franklin Roosevelt authorized the roundup of Japanese who had been placed on the A-B-C list. By nightfall on the seventh of December, 736 Japanese all along the West Coast had been transformed into fugitives. As government agents fanned out from Seattle, Washington, to San Diego, California, the arrests of listed individuals began. The wife of one man targeted by the FBI remembered how the "agents searched our small upper four-room flat, taking nothing" except her husband.[1] Another recalled the ransacking that occurred when the FBI searched his house: "They slit all the couches to see if anything was hidden."[2] In Hawaii, where fears of a follow-up Japanese attack were rampant, 345 Issei and 22 Nisei were under arrest by the evening of December 9. They were not alone, however. Anticipating imminent hostilities

with Japan's European allies, Germany and Italy, the government had authorized the detention of nationals from those
countries as well. Sitting in jail with the Japanese Hawaiians
were 19 Germans, 11 Italians, and 2 Italian Americans. A Japanese man picked up on December 8 found no sleep during his
first night of incarceration, because there was so much "turmoil
in the next room. . . . Germans and Italians were being hauled
in and the door kept banging as a new arrival was shoved in."[3]

Life for thousands upon thousands of men and women
identified with America's new enemies changed after December
7, and so did the public mood. In the immediate aftermath of
the Pearl Harbor strike, newspapers across the United States had
urged calm and warned against judging Japanese Americans
based on what their ethnic relatives had just perpetrated. A
mere two days later, the same *Los Angeles Times* that had tried
to assuage its readers' worst fears published an editorial that
claimed that the "entire Pacific Coast from British Columbia to
San Diego [is] prepared for possible raids."[4] Such statements by
reputable sources prompted many people, according to government reports, to consider everybody who looked Asian as bad,
and led Secretary of the Navy Frank Knox to advise President
Roosevelt that the immediate evacuation of at least Hawaii's
Japanese needed to be seriously debated.

Following the lead of the media and political establishment,
people went on the watch for enemies said to be lurking about
on land and at sea. Rumors began to spread about spies con-
tacting and passing vital intelligence to Japanese submarines
off the jagged shores and wind-swept beaches of California.
The sighting of four submarines and eight confirmed torpedo
attacks on American merchant ships from December 17 to 23
only heightened popular fears of an imminent Japanese move
against the West Coast. Public service announcements asking citizens to monitor local coves and sea cliffs for any sign
of Japanese agents signaling to vessels offshore aggravated
an already tense situation and encouraged average men and

women to become amateur sleuths on the lookout for enemy spies and saboteurs.

A grim revulsion toward reports, being received by the press in early 1942, of Japanese atrocities committed against American prisoners of war in the Pacific, further poisoned the atmosphere wherever Japanese and Japanese Americans interacted with their white neighbors. The Imperial Japanese Army had invaded the Philippines, Malaya, and the Dutch East Indies at the same time that the Japanese navy struck Pearl Harbor. Winning a series of early battles, the Japanese captured thousands of American, British, and Dutch soldiers. These unfortunate men were brutally treated by their captors. Prisoners of war were despised as cowards by the Japanese and deemed unworthy of proper treatment. As a result, they were subjected to starvation diets, forced marches, savage beatings, and summary execution (a type of killing in which the person is killed on the spot without a trial), usually by beheading. Stories of such horrors, when broadcast by the American media, reinforced prevailing stereotypes of Japanese as cruel, uncivilized, and, above all, untrustworthy. With increasing frequency, segments of the public began to demand that some sort of restrictive measures be placed on the Japanese population, at least in those areas most directly threatened by enemy military action.

Fears about the possibility of sabotage and espionage blended seamlessly with the stories of atrocities from the Pacific front to create a climate in which it became increasingly likely that some official policy might emerge concerning the wartime fate of Japanese Americans. If such a policy were developed, the man who would implement it would be Lieutenant General John L. DeWitt. A career military officer, DeWitt took charge of the Western Defense Command and the Fourth Army, headquartered at the Presidio of San Francisco, in December 1939. Forceful and outspoken, DeWitt made no attempt to hide his racist attitude toward nonwhites. The general used stereotypes to understand the world around him.

During World War II, about 75,000 American and Filipino soldiers were captured by Japanese troops in the Philippines. They were forced to march 60 miles (97 km) from Bataan to Japanese prison camps. Only one-fourth of the prisoners of war reached their destination in what is now known as the Bataan Death March.

Soon after arriving in San Francisco, he complained loudly that his command contained black troops and he wished to have only whites under his command.

Yet DeWitt's racial biases were initially less apparent regarding Japanese Americans, even in the immediate aftermath of Pearl Harbor. As voices on the streets of America and in the halls of Congress rose in support of some form of restriction on the freedom of Japanese Americans, DeWitt called for restraint and a reliance on standard security precautions. The general advised that risky Japanese aliens remain in detention. He also advocated greater scrutiny of Japanese-American social and political activity along with other seemingly common sense measures aimed at preventing sabotage and thwarting Japanese spy rings.

Along these lines, DeWitt recommended the confiscation of radio sets, cameras, and firearms from Japanese Americans, but he was not yet in favor of stronger action. Removing the tools of the spy trade, in the general's view, would suffice for the time being. Certainly, DeWitt did not advocate any kind of mass roundup or evacuation and incarceration of people, even in areas on the West Coast that the government deemed likely Japanese targets. DeWitt's argument against any wholesale effort to restrict, let alone remove, Japanese Americans was rooted in the notion that citizens were in an entirely different category than aliens. "An American citizen, after all," DeWitt said, "is an American citizen."[5]

THE OPINION TIDE TURNS

DeWitt and many others were not convinced in December 1941 that Japanese Americans posed enough of a threat to justify any action against them as a group. Attitudes, however, were rapidly shifting. The *Los Angeles Times* reflected the collective mood change sweeping over America in a January 1942 editorial that conceded that the time might have arrived for a broader detention policy, at least on the West Coast. Citing "the rigors of war," the newspaper lent its support to any future program of "proper detention of Japanese and their immediate removal from the most acute danger spots."[6] Others agreed. The mayor of Los Angeles, for example, expressed his backing for a roundup of Japanese Americans and attributed it to the fact that networks of spies and saboteurs already existed "in our own city" and that "each of our little Japanese friends will know his part" when the moment to strike arrived.[7] Following the mayor's lead, the Los Angeles Chamber of Commerce asked the Roosevelt administration to initiate a complete removal of Japanese from California.

The line on Japanese Americans taken by average citizens similarly changed dramatically in early 1942. Letters poured into President Roosevelt's office calling for a definitive policy regarding the Japanese community. A family in Southern California drafted a letter to Roosevelt demanding that he remove Japanese Americans because they were a "nasty, dirty, sneekie [sic] people."[8] A Seattle woman asked the president to "give some thought to ridding our beloved Country of these [Japanese] who hold no love or loyalty to our God, our ideals or our traditions, or our Government—They should *never* have been allowed here."[9] Other people succumbed to fits of paranoia in which they imagined Japanese plots to poison the region's food supply. These wild fantasies were more than enough justification, in the minds of many, for the Japanese to be driven out of the West. White farmers stoked such fears unceasingly, secure in the knowledge that valuable tracts of land held by their Japanese neighbors would come onto the market quickly and cheaply after any mass removal.

Always alert for any shift in their constituents' views, West Coast congressmen met in Washington, D.C., on January 30, 1942, to discuss ways in which to deal with the Japanese-American issue. The result was a unanimous decision to press the White House for a removal order along the lines of the one enacted by the Canadian government on January 14. The Canadian order first required Japanese nationals, and later all people of Japanese ancestry, to leave British Columbia. The primary difference between what the Western legislators sought and what the Canadians had done was that the American lawmakers would allow an initial period of voluntary evacuation. The congressmen even backed the development of a relocation program that would offer federal assistance, a new job, and a new home to all Japanese Americans who willingly left the West Coast for interior locations.

Yet what appeared reasonable and fair to some in Washington was interpreted as a sign of abject weakness by others. More than one congressman expressed dismay at their colleagues' penchant toward coddling the Japanese. And while the majority opinion on Capitol Hill still held for restraint, the ranks of those demanding the immediate evacuation of Japanese Americans were growing. These politicians wanted nothing to do with incremental voluntary programs that compensated participants for their cooperation. As one of them put it in a letter to Secretary of the Navy Frank Knox and FBI Director J. Edgar Hoover, "all Japanese, whether citizens or not, [should be] placed in inland concentration camps" at once.[10]

Back in their home states, as the Justice Department reported that January, the public strongly favored the mass evacuation of Japanese, citizen and non-citizen alike, even though Attorney General Francis Biddle made it clear that he did not know how any Japanese-American citizens could be removed and interned without openly violating their constitutional rights. These included the right of habeas corpus, in which a person had to be released from detention within days of arrest unless charged with a specific crime. U.S.-born Japanese Americans, Biddle contended, simply could not be interned, no matter how much popular support such a policy would have. Such tidy legal parameters, however, meant little to a public clamoring for action against a group many people saw as racial adversaries. A *San Francisco Chronicle* columnist summed up the perspective of the average American in 1942 when he wrote in support of "the immediate removal of every Japanese on the West Coast. . . . Herd 'em up, pack 'em off. . . . Personally, I hate the Japanese. And that goes for all of them."[11]

AN EXECUTIVE ORDER TAKES SHAPE

General DeWitt, like many other Americans, had a change of heart concerning Japanese Americans in early 1942. The change, however, was made more dramatic by the obvious contrast between his previous views and those he came to hold. At one time reluctant to consign Japanese-American citizens to internment, DeWitt claimed at the end of January to have "no confidence in their loyalty whatsoever"; for clarity's sake, he added, "I am speaking now of the native-born Japanese."[12] The

General John DeWitt recommended the evacuation of all Japanese from the West Coast, reporting to President Roosevelt that although no sabotage had been detected, this only proved that "a disturbing and confirming indication that such action will be taken." The president agreed and issued Executive Order 9066. Here, DeWitt *(right)* is awarded the Oak Leaf Cluster from Secretary of War Henry Stimson's successor, Robert Patterson, in 1945.

general then offered his approval to any measure that would enhance the security of his Western Defense Command, which he strongly felt was immediately threatened with attack, even though the chief of naval operations, Admiral Harold Stark, had stated that it was quite "impossible for the enemy to engage in a sustained attack on the Pacific Coast at this time."[13]

By early February, a fierce debate over the need for evacuation had broken out between the Justice Department, headed by Biddle, and the War Department. Although the secretary of war, Henry Stimson, opposed any Japanese relocation, his assistant secretary of war, John J. McCloy, and provost marshal, General Allen Gullion, wholeheartedly supported the idea. It was McCloy and Gullion who, at a February 3 meeting, began to discuss the notion of designating the entire West Coast as a military reservation, thereby allowing the federal government to forbid any and all civilians to reside there. The plan was to bar everyone from residence and then selectively issue return permits only to non-Japanese, effectively eliminating the Japanese-American presence. Asked for his opinion, DeWitt volunteered that no one, in California at least, would oppose a scheme of that sort. California's governor, Culbert Olsen, concurred. Californians, he said, "feel that they are living in the midst of enemies; they don't trust the Japanese, none of them."[14] Olsen's attorney general, Earl Warren—who would one day become California's governor before being appointed to the U.S. Supreme Court—reiterated this assumption during a February gathering of more than 150 sheriffs and public officials. The meeting ended with the officials openly advocating the immediate removal and internment of Japanese Americans in the interest of public safety.

Facing a solid front of support for evacuation, Biddle's Justice Department worried incessantly about "the danger of hysteria" and reported its concerns directly to Roosevelt.[15] In a memo to the president, Biddle reminded Roosevelt that "American-born Japanese, being citizens, cannot be apprehended or treated like alien enemies," but he conceded that a study nonetheless was under way to determine "whether, with respect to them, the writ of habeas corpus could be suspended."[16] Even FBI director Hoover, a man not usually given to reflection on matters of national security, responded to the plan for a security zone on the West Coast by expressing his belief that "the army was getting a bit hysterical."[17]

The War Department, despite the misgivings of Biddle and Hoover, merely increased the volume and intensity of its rhetoric. Gullion's confidant and War Department lawyer, Colonel Karl Bendetsen, warned ominously that "a substantial majority of Nisei bear allegiance to Japan . . . and at a proper time will engage in organized sabotage."[18] The safest course, Bendetsen argued, was to remove all Japanese from the West Coast and place them in relocation camps in the states of the Mountain West.

After the February 3 meeting, the process of moving toward mass evacuation gained momentum. McCloy told DeWitt to prepare a written proposal that would give the army the power to "exclude everyone—whites, yellows, blacks, greens—from [the West Coast] and license back into the area those whom we felt no danger from."[19] The assistant secretary meant all people except Japanese Americans. DeWitt, therefore, sat down to draft a tentative evacuation order secure in the knowledge that he had his superiors' approval and the backing of public opinion in the western states. Few would strenuously protest the removal and internment of Japanese Americans. A February 4 survey confirmed DeWitt's assumption. It found that, while most westerners felt that the government was doing enough to neutralize any threat from the Japanese-American population, fully 43 percent of the poll's respondents wanted stronger action, up to and including some form of mass detention.

Secretary of War Stimson was far less convinced that removal was in the best interests of the nation, at least from a legal standpoint. Stimson confided in his diary that he was "afraid [removal] will make a tremendous hole in our constitutional system."[20] Torn by indecision, the secretary of war shifted the responsibility for any action directly onto the shoulders of President Roosevelt. On February 11, Stimson sent a memo to Roosevelt and asked him if he would be willing to authorize the War Department to move Japanese, citizens and noncitizens alike, from restricted areas. Stimson's question elicited an oddly oblique response from Roosevelt, asking only that the War Department be reasonable in anything it did. However cryptic it seemed, this was taken as a yes, and the War Department proceeded with its preparations for the removal of Japanese Americans.

THE FINAL STEPS

DeWitt submitted his final recommendation, a document in reality drafted by Colonel Bendetsen, to Stimson's office on February 13. It stated clearly DeWitt's firm belief that the:

> Japanese race is an enemy race and while many second and third generation Japanese . . . have become "Americanized" their racial stains are undiluted. . . . Along the vital Pacific Coast over 112,000 potential enemies, of Japanese extraction, are at large today. . . . The Secretary of War [should] procure from the President direction and authority to designate military areas . . . from which, in his discretion, he may exclude all Japanese.[21]

Two days later, the conservative journalist Westbrook Pegler made the case for removal more succinctly but with no less racial hostility in a *Washington Post* editorial. "The Japanese in California," Pegler declared, "should be under armed guard to the last man and woman right now—and to hell with habeas corpus until the danger is over."[22]

Pressured by the combined weight of public opinion and the War Department, Biddle gave way. Over the strenuous objections of Edward Ennis, head of the Justice Department's Alien Enemy Control Unit and assistant to the attorney general, James H. Rowe, Biddle agreed to allow the implementation of a removal program to go forward. A presidential decree ordering the mass evacuation of Japanese Americans from the West Coast was now inevitable. It came on February 19, 1942, when Roosevelt signed Executive Order 9066. Giving his government agencies complete authority to round up and move Japanese Americans as a group, Roosevelt threw a mantle of legality over the forced relocation of more than 112,000 Americans based solely on their racial heritage, 70

EXECUTIVE ORDER 9066

President Franklin D. Roosevelt signed Executive Order 9066 in February 1942. The order essentially gave the War Department and Lieutenant General John DeWitt the authority to remove anyone they saw fit from the West Coast of the United States. Although the decree did not specifically mention Japanese Americans, it was clear to everyone that this one group was the primary target. Some Germans and Italians were detained, forced to relocate, or required to give up a business under the president's order, but only Japanese Americans were subjected to its provisions as an entire community. Responding to the Justice Department's early opposition to the War Department's efforts, the order explicitly directed all government agencies to assist not only in the removal of Japanese Americans but also in their relocation and internment. Following are the portions of 9066 that allow for mass relocation and compel agencies other than the War Department to offer assistance:

> . . . by virtue of the authority vested in me as President of the United States and Commander in Chief of the Army and Navy, I hereby authorize and direct the secretary of war and the military commanders whom he may from time to time designate . . .

percent of whom were native-born citizens.[23] DeWitt was ordered "to carry out [the] removal of individuals from areas where they are domiciled [living] . . . so far as consistent with national security."[24] The general, his racial biases seemingly vindicated, eagerly went to work to draw up a comprehensive plan for the internment, or confinement of tens of thousands of his fellow Americans.

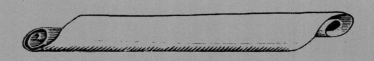

to prescribe military areas in such places and of such extent as he or the appropriate military commanders may determine, from which any and all persons may be excluded, and with such respect to which, the right of any person to enter, remain in, or leave shall be subject to whatever restrictions the secretary of war or the appropriate military commanders may impose in his discretion. The secretary of war is hereby authorized to provide for residents of any such area who are excluded therefrom, such transportation, food, shelter, and other accommodations as may be necessary . . . until other arrangements are made, to accomplish the purpose of this order. . . . I hereby further authorize and direct all executive departments, independent establishments, and other federal agencies, to assist the secretary of war or the said military commanders in carrying out this executive order, including the furnishing of medical aid, hospitalization, food, clothing, transportation, use of land, shelter, and other supplies, equipment, utilities, facilities, and services.*

* Lawson Fusao Inada, ed., *Only What We Could Carry: The Japanese American Internment Experience.* Berkeley, Calif.: Heyday Books, 2000, pp. 401–402.

Internment
Begins

For all of the attention focused on the West Coast of the United States, it was Hawaii that the Japanese planes had bombed on December 7. It was Hawaii that would be the most likely target of a Japanese follow-up raid or perhaps even a full-scale invasion. And it was Hawaii that laid claim to the largest community of Japanese-born Issei living anywhere in American territory. More than 150,000 Japanese called Hawaii home at the outbreak of World War II, each and every one of whom, according to the government logic of 1941–1942, could have been a spy or saboteur. It was hardly surprising, then, that the island territory drew the attention of the War Department very soon after President Franklin D. Roosevelt signed Executive Order 9066.

In fact, one week before Roosevelt's order was issued, General George Marshall, the Army chief of staff, recommended at least the partial evacuation of Hawaii's Japanese population. Writing to Roosevelt on behalf of the Joint Chiefs of Staff, Marshall urged the removal of no fewer than 20,000 Japanese to "a *concentration camp* on one of the Hawaiian Islands ... [or] a *concentration camp* located on the U.S. mainland."[1] This, to the general's mind, was the least that could be done to ensure the security of what had now become America's forward base in the war against Japan. Marshall made it clear to the president that the military leadership would prefer that all "Japanese residents of the Hawaiian Islands (whether U.S. citizens or aliens) be transported to the U.S. mainland and placed under guard at a concentration camp," but only if it were logistically feasible.[2] Otherwise, a partial evacuation of those Japanese believed to be the most dangerous would do.

Secretary of the Navy Frank Knox agreed with Marshall wholeheartedly. Hawaii, the secretary felt, and in particular Pearl Harbor, would never be completely safe while Japanese were free to remain where they were. "Personally," Knox wrote to Roosevelt, "I shall always feel dissatisfied with the situation until we get the Japanese out of Oahu...."[3] The president sympathized fully with Knox. No other U.S. port facility could replace Pearl Harbor; its safety and security were top concerns. The immediate presence of so many people whose loyalty was in question was a danger in and of itself. The American war effort could be compromised if enemy agents within the Japanese community successfully waged a campaign of sabotage against Pearl Harbor or the army bases and airfields around it. "Like you," Roosevelt replied to Knox, "I have long felt that most of the Japanese should be removed from Oahu to one of the other islands."[4]

Roosevelt, Knox, and the army all wanted some action taken with regard to Hawaii. Various plans for Japanese removal and relocation were floated in 1942, ranging from the detention of only those individuals posing obvious security threats to the total evacuation of the Japanese population. The latter was soon discarded as impractical and counterproductive. Neither the U.S. Navy nor the Merchant Marine had the shipping resources available to transport so many people so far, through waters prowled routinely by Japanese submarines. Moreover, the loss of nearly a third of Hawaii's workforce would cripple the island territory's economy and thus hinder, rather than help, the war effort. Strong opposition to removal by Hawaii's military governor, General Delos Emmons, sealed the case against mass relocation to the mainland, or anywhere else, for that matter. Despite Hawaii's large Japanese community, therefore, only 1,037 Japanese Hawaiians were detained and sent to mainland relocation centers during the war, not including 675 Issei held at special camps run by the Justice Department; a further 1,500 were interned locally at Sand Island near Honolulu.

SUPPORT—AND GROWING OPPOSITION

On February 25, 1942, the first Japanese Americans on the West Coast received orders to leave their homes. The Navy informed 500 families living on Terminal Island, near Los Angeles, that they had two days to move out of what was now considered to be a sensitive and restricted military area. Where they were supposed to go was neither told to the families nor deemed to be of any great concern to the military authorities evicting them. The first link in a long chain of evacuations, the Terminal Island removal provoked fear, confusion, and frustration among people who still thought of themselves as loyal Americans.

Support for the presidential order under which tens of thousands more Japanese would be forced from their homes came from many quarters. Nativist organizations like California's Sons and Daughters of the Golden West hailed Executive Order 9066 as a long-overdue measure to protect white political power and social privilege in the state. Similar groups, among them the California Joint Immigration Committee, sent representatives to testify before a House panel on removal, making

On February 19, 1942, President Roosevelt issued Executive Order 9066. This order declared certain areas of the United States as military areas from which "Foreign Enemy Ancestry" could be excluded. This led to the internment of some 120,000 ethnic Japanese, 11,000 ethnic Germans, and 3,000 ethnic Italians. Above, people read posted notices telling Japanese nationals and Japanese Americans to report for mandatory relocation.

it clear to the legislators their belief that extending citizenship to any Japanese in the first place had been a huge error. Committee members told Congress "a grave mistake was made when citizenship was granted to all born here, regardless of fitness or desire for such citizenship."[5] Racists and nativists all along the West Coast mocked the very idea that the Japanese could be or even wanted to be Americans.

These voices, however, were not the only ones raised in support of 9066. Even some Japanese organizations, chief among them the Japanese American Citizens League, came out in favor of a government policy that they considered at least partly justifiable and, if nothing else, an opportunity to demonstrate their loyalty in an unambiguous manner. Testifying before a House subcommittee in February 1942, the national treasurer of the JACL answered in the affirmative when asked if it was prudent to remove Japanese Americans from parts of the West. If the government felt it was necessary "from the danger standpoint, then all should be evacuated," the official stated.[6] The JACL's president went even further when the same question was put to him later, citing public safety as well as the demands of war: "Oh yes . . . there is not just national security" to think of, he said, but also the fact that Japanese Americans "may be subject to mob violence and otherwise if we are permitted to remain."[7] For his membership's own good, then, removal was warranted.

Yet despite such public demonstrations of approval, opposition to removal became increasingly apparent as implementation of 9066 moved forward. Critics, from civil liberties advocates to education experts, protested what they saw as a perversion of American justice and democracy. Within days of the announcement of the planned evacuation, President Roosevelt, in fact, received a protest letter signed by several prominent liberal figures, including the education reformer John Dewey and the philosopher Reinhold Niebuhr. The letter urged Roosevelt to reconsider his order, given that internment would closely approximate "the totalitarian theory of justice practiced by the Nazis in their treatment of the Jews."[8] One month later, the American Civil Liberties Union (ACLU), in a similar letter to the president, restated the claim that the

LIEUTENANT GENERAL JOHN L. DEWITT

Responsibility for the implementation of Executive Order 9066 and the removal of all Japanese from the West Coast fell to Lieutenant General John Lesesne DeWitt. Born at Fort Sidney, Nebraska, on January 9, 1880, DeWitt took a commission in the U.S. Army in 1898 and quickly found himself commanding troops in the Philippines during an insurrection in which racism figured prominently in several high-profile episodes of atrocity. After his service in the Philippines, DeWitt assumed duties along the Mexican border as U.S. troops hunted the Mexican revolutionary Francisco "Pancho" Villa. DeWitt eventually worked his way up to the rank of lieutenant colonel by the time he was sent to France in 1918, near the end of World War I.

Between the wars, DeWitt continued to rise through the officer ranks, becoming the army's quartermaster general in 1930. Seven years later, he was given command of the Army War College before his transfer to San Francisco and the Western Defense Command/ Fourth Army in 1939. His days fighting against brown-skinned Asians predisposed DeWitt to think in terms of extreme measures when America fought its next war in Asia in 1941. Besides his role in the internment program, DeWitt oversaw the defense of Alaska during the 1942 Japanese landings in the Aleutian Islands and played a small part in the 1944 Normandy invasion as part of the team responsible for deceiving the Germans as to the precise landing site for the Allied armies. After the Japanese surrender in 1945, DeWitt was appointed to lead the Army and Navy Staff College but retired after less than two years in the post. Acclaimed for his service during the war, he was promoted to the rank of full general in 1954. DeWitt died of heart failure in 1962 and was buried at Arlington National Cemetery. Many Japanese Americans would later quarrel with the decision to bury DeWitt among so many of America's heroes.

wholesale evacuation of Japanese Americans was a direct assault on American democracy. The provost of the University of California, Berkeley, expressed his sentiments even more bluntly, reminding Roosevelt that not a single person proposed to be relocated had committed any crime or act of espionage worthy of detention and internment.

Even the secretary of the treasury, Henry Morgenthau Jr., opposed the indiscriminate relocation of all Japanese. Using an economic argument, Morgenthau warned of the devastating financial losses to the Japanese-American community that would result from their removal and internment in the absence of any program allowing them to dispose of personal property, investments, and bank accounts. The secretary correctly anticipated a total loss of more than $500 million (in today's dollars) for families and businesses forced to liquidate their assets without proper government oversight. In response to Morgenthau's pleas, Roosevelt responded coldly, "Well, I am not concerned about that."[9]

THE PROCESS STARTS

Soon after Roosevelt signed Executive Order 9066, Attorney General Francis Biddle informed General DeWitt in San Francisco that the army could proceed with preparations for the evacuation of Japanese Americans without any further executive authority. DeWitt now had a free hand to exercise sweeping powers no single military commander had ever been given before in American history. On March 2, 1942, the general issued Public Proclamation No. 1, which divided his command into two military areas. Military Area No. 1 encompassed the western half of California, Oregon, and Washington, and southern Arizona. The remainder of those states was designated Military Area No. 2. Area No. 1 was further subdivided into two zones—one assigned prohibited status, the other restricted status. Lawful residence in or exclusion from either zone was decided at the sole discretion of the army, meaning DeWitt. As yet, no plans had been proposed for the mass evacuation of anyone, including Japanese Americans, but DeWitt made it clear to the media that "eventually orders will be issued requiring all Japanese, including those who are American born, to vacate all of Military Area No. 1."[10]

The process leading to internment gained momentum rapidly after DeWitt's proclamation. Within a week, Assistant Secretary of War John McCloy sent draft language for removal legislation to both houses of Congress. Five days later, Lieutenant Colonel Karl Bendetsen organized special War Department selection teams to scout and report on sites for future relocation centers. The teams took four days to settle on locations for at least 17 temporary assembly points and 10 permanent internment camps. Construction of the camps was to begin immediately, with an April 21 deadline for completion. Operation of the hastily constructed camps would fall under the jurisdiction of the newly created War Relocation Authority, an independent agency headed by Milton Eisenhower, the brother of General Dwight Eisenhower, which functioned under War Department supervision. Until the authority was fully up and running, responsibility for the assembly and relocation centers was assigned to the army's Wartime Civil Control Administration.

DeWitt now had the beginnings of an infrastructure for internment, but he lacked the legal authority to enforce his orders and proclamations; that could come only from Congress. Thus, on March 19, the House moved to enact Public Law 503, which gave the army and other agencies complete power to enforce the provisions of any decree related to Executive Order 9066 by setting explicit penalties for any defiance. There was pathetically little debate on the measure; it took only 10 minutes for the representatives to pass the law. The Senate needed a bit more time, but only because senators such as Democrat Robert Reynolds of North Carolina seized the opportunity to rant about how "Japanese pilots shot down over Pearl Harbor were found to be wearing Honolulu high school insignia and United States college rings," implicating American-born Japanese in the December 7 attack.[11] Senate approval was thus prefaced with a statement appearing to justify internment on the basis of a fictional connection between Japanese Americans and the Japanese enemy.

Congressional passage of Public Law 503 allowed DeWitt to issue Civilian Exclusion Order No. 1. DeWitt's order allowed for the removal of Japanese Americans from military areas—beginning with 50 families from Bainbridge Island, Washington—to the as-yet-unfinished relocation center at Manzanar in the California desert. Subsequently, the entire West Coast was divided into 107 evacuation districts, each responsible for funneling 1,000 Japanese into the emerging camp system. On March 26, DeWitt's hold on the Japanese population tightened still further as orders were given that prohibited any Japanese person from leaving the western military zone. The next day, Proclamation No. 3 was issued, announcing a curfew from 8:00 P.M. to 6:00 A.M. for "persons of Japanese ancestry" and restricting them to travel "not more than five miles from their place of residence."[12] More than 100,000 Americans were now captives in their own country.

EVACUATION AND ASSEMBLY

Trapped in their homes, Japanese Americans waited for the order to go. That order came in the form of exclusion notices posted throughout the removal districts on April 1. As outlined in the notices, the procedure for evacuation was planned to unfold over the course of a week. Notices appeared on day one. Days two and three were set aside for the registration of evacuees between 8:00 A.M. and 5:00 P.M. Processing was scheduled to take place on days four and five; actual physical removal was planned for days six and seven. The guidelines to ensure the smooth fulfillment of DeWitt's order were clear. Japanese Americans were to appear at the assigned location

To safeguard against any health concerns, evacuees were vaccinated as they registered at assembly centers for evacuation. Doctors and nurses were also of Japanese descent. The evacuees were later transferred to war relocation centers.

at a precise time, bringing with them only the most necessary belongings: "bedding and linen . . . toilet articles . . . extra clothing . . . knives, forks, spoons, plates, bowls, cups . . . essential personal effects."[13] Any other items had to be given away to neighbors or sold, almost always at a significant loss.

After local processing, Japanese-American evacuees were transferred to one of the assembly centers established as initial collection points for people en route to the relocation centers, which were being established at Tule Lake and Manzanar in California, Minidoka in Idaho, Heart Mountain in Wyoming,

Topaz in Utah, Poston and Gila River in Arizona, Granada in Colorado, and Rohwer and Jerome in Arkansas. Often situated at fairgrounds or racetracks, the assembly centers were unwelcoming places with few, if any, comforts or conveniences. The facility at Tanforan, a racetrack south of San Francisco, for example, lodged its residents in cramped stalls only recently vacated by horses. The consequences were predictable, as one Tanforan evacuee recalled:

> When we reached stall number 40, we pushed open the narrow door and looked uneasily into the vacant darkness. . . . Dust, dirt, and wood shavings covered the linoleum that had been laid over manure-covered boards, the smell of horses hung in the air, and the whitened corpses of many insects still clung to the hastily white-washed walls.[14]

Another unfortunate Tanforan inmate remembered how on "warm days it was unbearable in the stalls. . . . The stench of manure returned with the heat."[15]

As DeWitt's exclusion directive went into full effect, assembly centers filled with Japanese Americans. Homes throughout the West were shuttered, businesses were closed, farms were abandoned, and communities were torn apart as entire families, in many cases comprising several generations, were uprooted and forced to move. People who had known only San Francisco, San Diego, Los Angeles, Seattle, Portland, or perhaps one of the farm towns of California's Central Valley as home now had to become accustomed to new places far from anything familiar to them. Herded into one of the 13 assembly centers scattered along the West Coast, Japanese-American men, women, and children in the spring of 1942 waited anxiously for removal to become relocation.

Manzanar, Topaz, and Tule Lake

As tens of thousands of Japanese Americans languished in the assembly centers, the War Relocation Authority (WRA) worked feverishly to set up the internment camps that would be their new home for the duration of the war with Japan. War Department teams had already preselected eight possible sites in the western states and two in Arkansas by the time the WRA's Milton Eisenhower met with western governors at a conference held on April 7. In his address to the group, Eisenhower ill-advisedly asked for "any frank comments they might have regarding the proposed [internment] program."[1] He received much more than he bargained for. "If these people are dangerous on the Pacific coast, they will be dangerous here!" one governor thundered.[2] "If you bring Japanese into my state," another roared, "I promise you they will be hanging from every tree."[3] One after another, the governors made it clear to Eisenhower that their constituents hated Japanese Americans and simply would not tolerate their presence. Even if they were to remain locked behind barbed wire, the western governors flatly rejected the government's plan. In any case, as one governor put it, no state wanted to be "California's dumping ground."[4]

The criticism aimed at Eisenhower and the WRA was withering, but the internment program and the establishment of the relocation centers went forward according to the authority's schedule. Unlike the Justice Department camps, set up parallel to those of the WRA to incarcerate primarily suspect Issei and Japanese aliens, Eisenhower's centers were being erected exclusively to house Japanese Americans who were under no direct suspicion. The centers would also hold more than 2,000 Latin American Japanese who had been detained by their home governments and shipped to the United States for internment. Non-Japanese detainees were held either in Justice Department facilities or ones operated by the army. These together contained, by March 1942, no less than 1,393 Germans and 264 Italians. Smaller numbers of Germans and Italians were selectively detained in jails on individual warrants, and still others were forced to relocate or, as was the case with the father of the famous baseball player Joe DiMaggio, compelled to give up their businesses, in this instance, fishing. (Boats, according to the government's logic, could be used for espionage.)

The fact that some Germans and Italians were swept up by the government after the war began did nothing to change the reality that only Japanese Americans were subjected to mass evacuation and relocation without exception. And only Japanese Americans faced the very real possibility, as a racial group, that they would not see freedom again until the war with Japan ended. The destination for them all, alien and citizen alike, was a camp situated in a desolate and forbidding corner of America, a camp much like the one lying in the sand and rock of California's inland desert called Manzanar.

MANZANAR

Located some 225 miles (362 km) north of Los Angeles, in California's Owens Valley, the internment camp at Manzanar was the archetypal WRA relocation center. Set in the middle of a vast desert expanse, Manzanar experienced broiling summers as well as harsh, bitterly cold winters. The camp covered nearly 6,000 acres (2,428 ha) of land, owned by the city of Los Angeles, and at its height of operation had a population of more than 10,000 Japanese Americans, mostly from southern California. Opened in March 1942 as a Wartime Civil Control Administration assembly center, Manzanar was transformed into an internment camp in June, thus coming under the jurisdiction of the WRA.

Like the other nine WRA internment camps, Manzanar quickly evolved into a self-contained Japanese-American community, complete with a school, a library, an infirmary, churches, a camp newspaper—the *Manzanar Free Press*—athletic teams, and industries ranging from a camouflage net manufacturing shop to a mattress factory. The camp also had all of the social conflicts found in any social setting. In fact, perhaps to a greater extent than at other relocation centers, Manzanar experienced heightened social tensions between divergent groups of people. The traditional Japanese divisions between Issei, Nisei, and Kibei were apparent, with the understandable generational gap between elderly Japanese and their more-Americanized offspring. Issei parents, more Japanese in their outlook, often quarreled with their Nisei children, who felt few, if any, ties to the imperial homeland. Caught in the middle were native-born Kibei who had been raised in America but culturally and academically educated in Japan.

The Manzanar community also had to reconcile the competing political loyalties of its members, a process that often ended in hostility and occasionally violence. The presence in the camp of an ultranationalist organization known as the Black Dragon was particularly divisive and disruptive.

Many evacuees had only a week to decide what to do with their homes and other possessions, pack, and take only what they could carry to internment camps like Manzanar *(above)*. Located in the Owens Valley between the Sierra Nevada on the west and the Inyo Mountains on the east, about 10,000 Japanese Americans were crowded into 504 barracks organized into 36 blocks.

Composed primarily of disillusioned, angry young Kibei, the Black Dragon was dedicated to undermining U.S. government authority within the camp and the American war effort being supported in part by camp labor. Black Dragon toughs routinely harassed and bullied anyone suspected of aiding the camp managers or the army in any way. Black Dragon leaflets appeared early on in the camp, "urging Nisei not to be fools, to stop working on war equipment." One former internee remembered, "Rumors of all sorts were circulating, including one that the Black Dragon had prepared a 'death list.'"[5]

The hostility generated by these and other social, cultural, and political resentments only added to the ones arising naturally out of the frustrations that accompanied the humiliation of internment itself. Together, all this created an atmosphere at Manzanar that was ripe to protest and, in December 1942, to a near uprising, when guards had to use armed force to prevent physical attacks against *inu*, men who worked with the camp administration. Literally translated as "dog" but meaning "informer," the word *inu* was applied to anyone suspected of collaborating with or spying for the camp overseers and served to mark the bearer as a target for Black Dragon thugs and others. The December incident ended with gunfire and the deaths of two internees, one of whom was a 17-year-old girl.

Living conditions at Manzanar only exacerbated the problems within the barbed wire. At all of the relocation centers, Manzanar included, Japanese-American families were assigned to "apartments" that were in reality little more than cramped, uncomfortable enclosures, minimally better than those at the assembly centers like Tanforan. Each family had a living space no larger than 20 feet by 24 feet, or 480 square feet (6 by 7.3 meters, or 44.5 square meters). Partitions rather than actual walls separated one "apartment" from another; none had running water or any indoor plumbing. Common descriptions of Manzanar's bleak barracks-style housing speak of "bare floors, blanket partitions, one [light] bulb in each compartment dangling from a roof beam."[6] Food was cooked and served in mess halls and was notoriously bland and often unhealthy. Food sanitation was so poor at Manzanar that internees regularly suffered from stomach disorders and diarrhea: "The 'Manzanar runs' became a condition of life," one internee said, "and you only hoped that when you rushed to the latrine, one would be in working order."[7] Those latrines, shared in common by an entire block, provided no privacy and were so badly maintained that some government health officials were shocked that disease did not become epidemic.

THE JEWEL OF THE DESERT
However typical, Manzanar was only one of 10 camps. By October 1942, 111,999 Japanese Americans had been warehoused in it and the other nine WRA centers, of which just one received

a semiofficial motto. Far to the east of Manzanar, in Utah, was an internment camp that proudly announced to its inmates that they were being held in the "Jewel of the Desert"—Topaz. Sitting on 19,800 acres (8,012 ha) of Great Basin scrubland, 140 miles (225 km) south of Salt Lake City, Topaz was one of the largest WRA facilities, but at its height the camp interned a mere 8,130 people, nearly all of whom had come from northern California by way of the Tanforan assembly center. A journey of roughly 1,000 miles (1,600 km), the trip by rail from Tanforan to Topaz, in the words of one unwilling traveler, "was a nightmare that lasted two nights and a day. . . . Many became train sick and vomited. The children cried from restlessness. At one point on the way, a brick was thrown into one of the cars."[8]

Forced to endure the same conditions as the Manzanar internees, those at Topaz experienced the same range of emotional upheavals and social disruptions. Living at an elevation of 4,600 feet (1,402 m), Japanese Americans at Topaz struggled through summers during which temperatures rose to 106°F (41°C) and shivered during winters when the mercury fell to -30°F (-34°C). Nature, however, represented only one source of hardship for those locked away in the Utah camp. The routines of camp life led to widespread boredom for the young and often clinical depression for the old. Sharing camp facilities, such as toilets and showers, embarrassed everyone. A dreadful lack of privacy strained social bonds and sowed the seeds of discord between individuals and entire families. "As time went on," according to a former internee, "the residents of Topaz began to release their frustrations on others. . . . Internal squabbling spread like [a] disease."[9]

Politics, as at the other camps, became another point of irritation at Topaz. Competing loyalties tore at the community. Issei labored to retain their Japanese selves and ties to the cultural traditions of their birthplace; Nisei strove just as mightily to prove their Americanness and allegiance to the United States and its culture and traditions. Kibei, more so than at Manzanar, wavered between these poles, at times drifting toward a more

REMEMBERING POSTON

Camp life put tremendous stress on individuals and families alike. Men, women, and children struggled daily to maintain their personal and collective identities in the absence of those institutions and structures that had given them a sense of themselves before evacuation. Families, in particular, were hard pressed by camp conditions to preserve the customs and traditions that underlay Japanese-American culture. At every relocation center, family cohesion was compromised as generations drifted apart and children increasingly challenged the hierarchies around them. Fathers became peculiarly sensitive to their roles as heads of household; mothers defended their positions as caregivers. All the while, children, especially teenagers, asserted an independence newly found in camp environments that swept away a large degree of the power exercised by their parents. These conflicts played out in similar fashion at each camp, including the one at Poston, Arizona. There, the fabric of Japanese-American family life was subjected to tensions that often threatened to tear it apart, as described by Helen Shishino, a former Poston internee. A young girl at the time, Shishino recalls how her father reacted to one of the challenges her family encountered:

> My parents were Issei and so, when we got to camp everybody had, you know, picnic tables. . . . One family would be assigned to one table, and so that's the way it was—eating breakfast, lunch, and dinner with your family. But then, later on when everybody got to know everybody, they found that the boys, teenage boys, would be eating at one table, and they were making a whole bunch of noise, and all the teenage girls were eating at another table, and the family unit was breaking down. My father was a block manager, and so the parents would complain how

(continues)

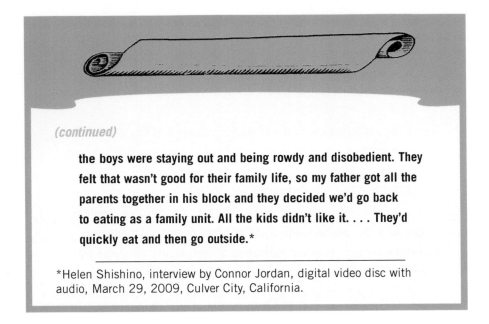

(continued)

the boys were staying out and being rowdy and disobedient. They felt that wasn't good for their family life, so my father got all the parents together in his block and they decided we'd go back to eating as a family unit. All the kids didn't like it. . . . They'd quickly eat and then go outside.*

---

*Helen Shishino, interview by Connor Jordan, digital video disc with audio, March 29, 2009, Culver City, California.

pro-Japanese attitude before assuming a more pro-American patriotic stance. These divisions grew and sharpened over the early months of internment and generated lasting animosities that, while generally empty of violent content, were full of psychologically and socially destructive potential.

THE SEGREGATION CENTER

By early 1943, it had become clear that the tide of the war in the Pacific had turned in favor of the United States and that the West Coast was no longer in any danger of Japanese attack. Prominent figures inside and outside of the government began to reconsider the propriety and usefulness of the internment program. Proposals were put forward regarding the initiation of some sort of incremental release of internees. The manpower demands of global warfare highlighted the need for exactly the type of fit, well-motivated young American men who now sat idle in the camps. Indeed, many military officials saw an untapped pool of potential soldiers among the throngs of Japanese-American youths at places like Manzanar and Topaz. Local and national economies would also receive a much-needed boost from the return of Japanese-American laborers, skilled workers, and businessmen. Yet, before any release could be considered, the Roosevelt administration needed some way of distinguishing between the loyal and disloyal in the camp population. The solution, the government believed, was a questionnaire designed to establish an internee's willingness to declare his devotion to the United States. (It was taken for granted that the proposed questionnaire would be aimed at men by virtue of their suitability for military service or their roles as heads of household.) Entitled "Application for Leave Clearance," the form, which was eventually drawn up as a companion to a second questionnaire designed specifically for men of military age, implied a general release for anyone completing it and should have been eagerly accepted by the camp residents. In practice, however, the questionnaire presented its readers with a troubling dilemma. Among the questions were two problematic queries regarding national affiliation and readiness to serve in the armed forces. Question 27 asked whether the applicant would be willing to serve in either a combatant or support role in the U.S. Army; Question 28 demanded a reply to the following: "Will you swear unqualified allegiance to the United States of America and forswear any form of allegiance or obedience to the Japanese emperor, or any other foreign government, power, or organization?"[10] These two seemingly innocuous questions threw the camps into turmoil as no other issue had done and caused an uproar among Japanese Americans perhaps exceeded only by Executive Order 9066 itself.

Question 27 obviously demanded that young Japanese Americans respond directly to a call for service and sacrifice from precisely the same government that had imprisoned them. Answering "yes" put the respondent in the position of possibly having to shed blood for his jailers, while "no" immediately indicated either cowardice or disloyalty. Question 28 assumed that the respondent had been affiliated in the past with an enemy power, something patently untrue for American-born citizens, thus invalidating either an affirmative or negative reply by a Nisei. The same question put Issei in the unenviable position of renouncing their Japanese citizenship with a "yes" while still being barred from becoming naturalized American citizens. These respondents, therefore, would be left as people without a country. Marking a "no" answer to Question 28, on the other hand, would brand them disloyal, as it would any Nisei or Kibei who did likewise. Eventually, more than 5,000 Nisei and Kibei resolved this problem by renouncing their citizenship; most Issei simply checked the "no" box and prepared to accept whatever label the government hung on them.

In either case, the wrong answers to Questions 27 and 28 on the leave clearance form put one on the road to the segregation center at Tule Lake, a camp reserved for Japanese Americans deemed to be incorrigibly disloyal. Located among the lava beds of northern California, near the Oregon border, Tule Lake opened in May 1942 and housed evacuees from Sacramento and various parts of Washington and Oregon. Initially, no difference existed between Tule Lake and any other center, but, following a series of disturbances and protests concerning Question 28, the camp was redesignated as a segregation center. Its 26,000 acres (10,521 ha) of sagebrush became a repository for Japanese-American internees who either said "no" to Question 28 or refused to respond at all. "Camp Tule Lake was an internment camp converted into a maximum-security camp for 'disloyals,'" former inmate and future television star George Takei recalled. "The fence was heavy wire mesh. . . . The guard towers were turrets equipped with machine guns. The outer perimeter was patrolled by a half-dozen trucks and armored jeeps."[11] Such high security was deemed necessary to contain safely the "disloyals" as well as any Issei or Nisei who had expressed a desire to be repatriated to Japan after the war. Collecting together two clearly disaffected groups seemed logical in the spring of 1943, but it resulted in the creation of a camp atmosphere uniquely conducive to hostility and unrest.

By November 1943, the government questionnaire had been in circulation for months, and Tule Lake had been transformed into a cauldron of resentment and discontent. On November 1, the WRA chief, Dillon Myer, who had replaced Milton Eisenhower in the summer of 1942, visited the camp. Angered by Myer's presence and convinced that they were being treated in a discriminatory fashion even by WRA standards, a group of Tule Lake internees scuffled with camp guards on November 4 over the rumored diversion of food rations to other camps. By the time the uproar subsided, martial law had been declared at Tule Lake, and 350 internees had been arrested.

After the November riot, Tule Lake gained a reputation as a den of not only traitors and spies but also troublemakers. The riot appeared to reinforce the worst stereotypes of Japanese Americans as dangerous and unpredictable and led many people to conclude that internment had been warranted after all. "This is no occasion for sentimentality," the *New York Times* wrote after the Tule Lake protest. "We can't give leeway to possible spies and saboteurs simply because we want to believe that human nature, including that which is wrapped in saffron-colored skin, is inherently good."[12] The *Los Angeles Times* similarly took a hard line in response to the unrest at Tule Lake. Soon after Myer concluded his tour, the *Los Angeles Times* published a questionnaire asking its readers whether Japanese Americans should be permanently excluded from the West Coast—by a margin of ten to one, the respondents answered "yes."[13]

Discontent, frustrations, and despair punctuated the lives of Japanese Americans at each and every one of the WRA camps. Heart Mountain, Poston, and Gila River (originally under the jurisdiction of the Office of Indian Affairs because it was located on an Indian reservation) all experienced periods of unrest and occasional violence. Only Minidoka enjoyed relative peace, because of the unusually considerate and solicitous camp administrators and lenient security officials. Elsewhere—at Jerome, Rohwer, and Granada, for example—friction between internees and a bitterness born of tedium and hopelessness were commonplace. Frequent attempts at distraction, like baseball games, dances, and theatrical presentations, did little

In an attempt to make the most of a bad situation, internees developed sports clubs, boys and girls organizations, music, dance, and other recreational programs. They also published their own newspapers and worked in the camp. Above, young internees are at a dance party at the Tule Lake relocation camp.

to relieve the long-term pressures of camp life. Self-conscious efforts at community building that included publishing newspapers, attending school, or going to church did not erase the fact that they were imprisoned for no reason other than race. The shame and humiliation felt by many internees could not be assuaged through diversions and cosmetic normality. Only a reinvigorated sense of Americanness and release from internment held out hope to Japanese Americans of regaining their place in the national society and culture. Opportunities for both were soon to present themselves, as the American economy and war effort awoke to the forgotten potential of Japanese-American labor and military.

The Struggle Against Internment

The leave-clearance questionnaire that appeared in the internment camps in 1943 held out hope to many Japanese Americans that their long ordeal might soon be over. Yet, for some of them, the fight to end internment had already begun in the courts in a series of legal challenges to the basic concepts that underlay the program. Prompted by a profound sense that justice was central to the American way of life, a tiny minority of Japanese-American men and women willingly engaged in acts of civil disobedience designed specifically to force judges and eventually the justices of the United States Supreme Court to rule definitively on the constitutionality of internment. They hoped to bring the issue of the internment of law-abiding citizens to the front of the discussion concerning civil rights during wartime. Their names were Minoru Yasui, Gordon Hirabayashi, Fred Korematsu, and Mitsuye Endo.

Born in Oregon to Japanese immigrant parents, Minoru "Min" Yasui was educated as a lawyer at the University of Oregon. Yasui took great pride in his law degree and the training he had received at college to become an Army Reserve officer. Unable to find work at a law firm after graduating in 1939, Yasui took a job at the Japanese consulate in Chicago and registered as a foreign agent, as the law required. When Japan attacked the United States on December 7, 1941, Yasui immediately resigned and rushed to enlist in the army, but he was denied a commission because of his race and because he had worked for the Japanese government. Only days later, Yasui's father, who had encouraged his son to join the armed forces because his "country is at war and needs you,"[1] was arrested and sent from the family's home in Oregon to a Justice Department camp in Montana.

His father's arrest, combined with his inability to serve his country, drove Yasui to return to Oregon and openly challenge the government's restrictive policies. The particular measure Yasui had in mind was the 8:00 P.M. to 6:00 A.M. curfew imposed on Japanese Americans by General John L. DeWitt. At exactly 11:00 P.M. on March 28, 1942, three hours into the curfew, Yasui took a walk and then turned himself into the Portland police for violating the order. Yasui defiantly claimed that the very idea of a curfew on innocent Americans "infringed on my rights as a citizen."[2] After some time in jail and a lengthy trial, Yasui was convicted of violating Proclamation No. 3 and was sentenced to a year in prison and a $5,000 fine.

Yasui's indignation arose out of his rejection by the army and his father's detention. Gordon Hirabayashi, on the other hand, fought the government solely based on his personal conviction that internment was inherently unjust. A University of Washington senior at the time, Hirabayashi strode into a Seattle FBI office in May 1942 and announced his refusal to register for evacuation. "This order for mass evacuation of all persons of Japanese descent," Hirabayashi argued in a written statement, "denies the right to live. . . . Hope for the future is exterminated. Human personalities are poisoned."[3] Offered release on bail four days later, Hirabayashi chose to remain in jail.

His case went to trial that October. Claiming that an exclusion order applying to an entire community violated the Fifth Amendment guarantee of due process, Hirabayashi's lawyer moved for dismissal. The judge in the case responded by denying the motion and instead launched into a lecture on the relationship between evacuation and the war with Japan. The jury took only 10 minutes to return a verdict of guilty. Hirabayashi received a 90-day sentence; his lawyer filed an appeal immediately, having every intention of moving the case before the Supreme Court at the earliest possible moment.

AMERICANS V. THE UNITED STATES: KOREMATSU AND ENDO

Yasui and Hirabayashi sought to use their cases to challenge the constitutionality of the core principles behind Executive Order 9066. Fred Korematsu, for his part, simply wanted to stay out of an assembly center to be close to a young woman he found irresistibly attractive. Korematsu was arrested in San Leandro, California, on May 30, 1942, after weeks of hiding under an assumed name and claiming to be Chinese. Rejected by the army after Pearl Harbor, Korematsu had taken a part-time job as a welder and had done his best to remain inconspicuous. Well aware that his various ruses would not hold out forever, Korematsu had gone as far as to have plastic surgery to make himself look less Asian.

Korematsu's efforts, however, proved fruitless in the end. His love interest rebuffed his advances, and his attempts at disguise failed. "The way I got caught," Korematsu later recalled, "was that I went into a drugstore to get some cigarettes and the pharmacist recognized me. He was the one who called the police."[4] Charged with violating the government's exclusion order, Korematsu was convicted in September 1942 and

On January 15, 1998, then-U.S. president Bill Clinton awarded the Presidential Medal of Freedom, the nation's highest honor, to Fred Korematsu. During World War II, instead of following orders requiring Japanese Americans to report to relocation centers, Korematsu challenged the legality of the order.

sentenced to five years probation and released on bail. He was quickly seized by military police officers and escorted directly to the Tanforan assembly center.

Mitsuye Endo was already sitting in one of the stalls at Tanforan even as she was being tried. A former California

Department of Motor Vehicles employee, Endo had lost her job a month after Pearl Harbor and had been forced into the assembly center's stables. There she was approached by an attorney for the Japanese American Citizens League who simply "couldn't understand why innocent citizens were being treated this way."[5] Endo was offered the opportunity to become a test case for a challenge to the evacuation order. As a Nisei, it was argued that Endo's detention violated the rule of habeas corpus and was thus illegal. By July 1942, Endo's lawyers had filed a petition for her release and a hearing was scheduled. During the court proceedings, the government's attorneys urged the presiding judge to dismiss the petition on the grounds that Japanese Americans, as a group, could not be trusted and therefore had to remain in detention for the duration of the war with Japan. More than a year passed before the court ruled, without comment, against Endo.

THE HIRABAYASHI DECISION

The case of *Hirabayashi v. United States* compelled the Supreme Court to explain how American citizens could be legally discriminated against based solely on their racial or ethnic background. Theoretically, such discrimination was contrary to the American tradition of equality under the law and the U.S. Constitution. The court in *Hirabayashi*, therefore, had to outline the precise circumstances under which Japanese Americans could be singled out for restrictions that applied to no other group, even those directly related by ancestry to the nation's other enemies during World War II, Germany and Italy. The justices' presentation of a rationale for

(continues)

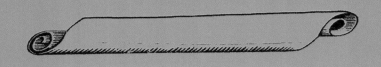

(continued)

upholding the curfew and other restrictive measures challenged by Gordon Hirabayashi in 1942 began with an affirmation of the rights of racial minorities:

> Distinctions between citizens solely because of their ancestry are by their very nature odious to a free people whose institutions are founded upon the doctrine of equality. For that reason, legislative classification or discrimination based on race alone has often been held to be a denial of equal protection. We may assume that these considerations would be controlling here were it not for the fact that the danger of espionage and sabotage, in time of war and threatened invasion, calls upon the military authorities to scrutinize every relevant fact bearing on the loyalty of populations in the danger areas. Because racial discriminations are in most circumstances irrelevant and therefore prohibited, it by no means follows that, in dealing with the perils of war, Congress and the Executive are wholly precluded from taking into account those facts and circumstances . . . which may place citizens of one ancestry in a different category from others. . . . We cannot say that these facts and circumstances, considered in the particular war setting, could afford no ground for differentiating citizens of Japanese ancestry from other groups in the United States. The fact alone that attack on our shores was threatened by Japan rather than another enemy power set these citizens apart from others who have no particular association with Japan . . .*

---

*Henry Steele Commager, *Documents of American History*, Volume II. New York: Appleton-Century-Crofts, 1958, p. 649.

The cases of Yasui, Hirabayashi, Korematsu, and Endo all reached the Supreme Court in 1943. The Yasui and Hirabayashi verdicts were soon upheld, notwithstanding dissenting opinions such as the one by Justice Frank Murphy regarding the Hirabayashi case: "This gigantic roundup of no less than 70,000 American citizens . . . is so utterly inconsistent with our ideals and traditions, and in my opinion so contrary to constitutional sanctions, that I cannot give my assent."[6] The court did not issue a ruling in the Korematsu and Endo cases until December 1944. Korematsu's case verdict was upheld, but the decision in Endo's was overturned and the right of habeas corpus applied not only to Endo but, by extension, to all Japanese Americans then interned by the government. By that late date, however, a process of general release for internees had been implemented and was well under way.

THE EARLY RELEASES

Not long before Fred Korematsu was arrested in San Leandro, President Roosevelt received a visit from his closest adviser, Harry Hopkins. Hopkins told Roosevelt about a request from Robert Gordon Sproul, the president of the University of California, Berkeley. Sproul had appealed to Hopkins for the release of Japanese-American college students whose studies had been interrupted by internment. Hopkins had never supported indiscriminate internment anyway; now he argued vigorously that keeping some of the brightest young minds in America behind barbed wire made no sense. After the war, Hopkins contended, a reconstituted Japanese-American community would need intelligent, well-educated leaders to merge once again into the mainstream of American life. Hearing such a plea from his most trusted political adviser, Roosevelt relented and ordered that "qualified American-born Japanese students . . . be enabled to continue their education in inland institutions."[7] While not allowed to return to their West Coast schools, Japanese-American students were at least free to walk into classrooms in America's heartland and at selected locations on the East Coast.

The University of Nebraska was one university that eagerly opened its doors to released students. Admission, however, was only the first hurdle faced by former internees. While university administrators and faculty members were welcoming to the new students, their peers often were not. Fearful of their white classmates' prejudices and suspicions, Japanese-American students strove mightily to fit in and, above all, maintain a low profile. One such student wrote home from Nebraska to relate how "all of us [Japanese] have tried to avoid being seen in conspicuous groups and have tried to spread out as much as possible."[8] A female internee, released to attend Wellesley College in Massachusetts, assured her parents in a letter that life beyond the camps was difficult but not unbearable. "I haven't noticed that my being [Japanese] has made much difference on the campus itself. Oh yes, I had one nasty 'grilling.' One student accused practically all Japanese in this country of being in some way connected with the 'sabotage and espionage network.'" She concluded by writing "people stare at me, but not so much as to make me feel uncomfortable."[9]

Hopkins had urged student releases out of a concern for the future. Secretary of the Interior Harold Ickes was more narrowly focused on the present. Specifically, Ickes saw large numbers of skilled workers sitting idly in internment camps while the American economy struggled to meet the needs of a nation at war. Ickes pushed the Roosevelt administration to enact economic-release policies, however partial, that would permit Japanese-American workers to re-enter the labor force. Defending his position in the pages of the *New York Times* in June 1942, Ickes stated his case in clear, concise terms. "We need competent help very badly," he said, "and these are highly skilled workers."[10] Considering the material requirements of global warfare, Roosevelt conceded the point to Ickes and allowed Japanese-American workers, especially farm laborers and factory workers, conditional release to aid the war effort.

While in the camps, internees worked at various jobs including digging irrigation canals, raising farm animals, and tending acres of fruits and vegetables. About 10,000 people at the 10 camps were allowed to leave temporarily to harvest sugar beets in Idaho, Montana, Wyoming, and Utah.

Following the government's decision in 1942, some 10,000 Japanese Americans were soon released from assembly centers to bring in crops throughout the West, on the condition that they would proceed to internment camps after the harvest. The policy proved so successful that it was repeated each season thereafter. An example of the contribution made by such partial releases was apparent in the productivity of the Utah-Idaho Sugar Company. The company hired 3,500 internees in 1942 to help harvest the western sugar beet crop. With the indispensable help of Japanese hands and backs, the firm eventually produced more than 100 million pounds (45 million kilograms) of sugar for the domestic market and shipment overseas.

LEAVE CLEARANCE

Students were released to attend their universities; workers were allowed freedom to bring in America's food crops. As the obvious successes in these two areas became apparent, the leave-clearance program was being instituted. Once the initial ambivalence concerning Questions 27 and 28 on the leave-clearance questionnaire had been overcome, by segregating those who refused to answer "yes" to both, the process of developing some kind of general release framework and protocol continued. Steps were being taken to release and resettle a small number of Japanese Americans to widely dispersed towns and cities primarily throughout the Plains and the Midwest, as a trial run for the day when the war would end and the internees would be freed. War Relocation Authority officials anticipated opening six regional resettlement offices and 35 subregional offices to handle the transition from internment to a new life, first for the initial groups and later for the general population. WRA head Dillon Myer went to work very early, promoting the general concept of release itself as well as his agency's specific program. By March 1943, Myer was busily, if a bit ironically, telling skeptical Americans not to fear the release of Japanese Americans, because "the evacuees were charged with nothing except having Japanese ancestors."[11] Moreover, the director warned, continued wholesale internment would hand the Imperial Japanese propaganda machine a bonus by allowing it to claim with some legitimacy "that this nation preaches democracy and practices racial discrimination."[12] Lastly, a consensus had begun to emerge inside the WRA that held further internment to be too costly and detrimental to the wartime economy and perhaps even the postwar economy.

For all these reasons, Myer argued publicly and to the president that the time for change had arrived. Through Secretary of War Henry Stimson, Myer proposed three release options to the president. Roosevelt could simply close the internment camps and reopen the West Coast for Japanese residence. Less dramatically, the president could order an acceleration and expansion of the leave-clearance program. Roosevelt could split the difference between these two alternatives by closing the camps while leaving the West Coast restrictions in place. Significantly, all three options included provisions for releasing and drafting men of military age. As the president pondered his choices, his wife, Eleanor, added a maternal element to her husband's deliberations by supporting the broadest possible release at the earliest possible date. The first lady, after an April 1943 visit to the Gila River relocation center, wrote that camp life not only disrupted family life but also distorted childhood in particular. In an interview with the *Los Angeles Times*, she deplored the effects of internment on children and declared "the sooner we get young Japanese out of the camps the better."[13]

President Roosevelt, by mid-1943, knew well the opinions of a wide range of people in favor of release. But he also heard echoes of earlier calls for the most restrictive policies the law allowed and continued internment of the entire Japanese-American population. Testifying before a House subcommittee in April 1943, Governor Earl Warren of California warned legislators that, if the internees "are released, no one will be able to tell a saboteur from any other [Japanese person]."[14] The same congressional panel heard from witnesses who made outrageous claims about the proposed release: The WRA, it was said, was advocating for Japanese Americans because it was pro-Axis; the WRA planned to let internees escape and engage in a sabotage campaign; pro-Japanese gangs, active in the camps, were set to be freed to roam at will; released internees had arranged to gain access to a hidden cache of weapons in the California desert and would use it to supply a Japanese invasion force. Perhaps most ridiculous was the charge that a secret Japanese army had trained in the camps and awaited release to complete its mission of attacking America from the inside. Ludicrous though they were, such paranoid delusions reflected a strong current of public opinion wary of ending a program that had been touted a year earlier as vital to national security.

Roosevelt took the views of the public, however absurd on occasion, very seriously. Key administration officials nonetheless continued to press for a comprehensive and coherent release policy from the White House. Attorney General Francis Biddle, in a memorandum to the president, stated bluntly his belief that the "current practice of keeping loyal American citizens in concentration camps . . . is dangerous and repugnant to the principles of our government."[15] Harold Ickes, with the added weight of support from General Delos Emmons, the new Western Defense Command chief, likewise pressured Roosevelt to end the internment of Japanese Americans. Ickes put no stock in the rantings of "professional race-mongers."[16] Yet what impressed Roosevelt most deeply and ultimately led him to conclude that ending internment was in the nation's best interest was the argument that thousands of potential soldiers were wasting away in the drafty barracks and lonely dregs of the camps, while the manpower needs of the army were on the rise. Although total closure of the relocation centers and resettlement still lay at a distance in the future, Roosevelt came to the decision in 1943 to offer conditional release to any Japanese-American man ready, willing, and able to serve his country. The president subsequently approved the formation of an all-Japanese-American combat unit to fight overseas for the liberty denied them at home.

Citizen Soldiers

Two weeks after the attack on Pearl Harbor, the Japanese-American newspaper *Rafu Shimpo* made a plea to the nation. Arguing that Japanese Americans were as patriotic as anyone else, the newspaper's editor called on his "fellow Americans to give us the opportunity to serve our cause in the front ranks [of the army] . . . where danger is most conspicuous."[1] Over the next few months, *Rafu Shimpo* repeated its demand that Japanese Americans be allowed to demonstrate their loyalty by serving in the armed forces. Like most of its readers, the paper recognized the connection between patriotism and the military in American culture and the public imagination. "We want this straight for the record," a February 1942 editorial announced. "We know with confidence that we can be of service to the cause of American victory."[2]

Such certainty, however, did not extend much further than the boundaries of the Japanese-American community. Most non-Japanese had little faith in the trustworthiness, let alone the fighting capabilities, of men so closely associated with the enemy that had struck at Pearl Harbor. From December 1941 through the following spring, moreover, America's war against Japan was fought on the defensive. With the exception of Lieutenant Colonel Jimmy Doolittle's air raid against Tokyo in April 1942 and the inconclusive naval engagement in the Coral Sea the following month, the United States had ceded the initiative to the Japanese, choosing to concentrate its energies on defending Hawaii and the West Coast from a possible follow-up attack to the one at Pearl Harbor. As long as the Japanese had the upper hand strategically, few if any Americans were inclined to accept the notion of Japanese Americans in uniform.

Yet this situation changed dramatically in June 1942, when an American aircraft carrier battle group crushed a Japanese carrier strike force sent to capture Midway Island at the extreme western end of the Hawaiian Islands chain. During this one sea battle, four of the six Japanese aircraft carriers that had launched the planes used in the Pearl Harbor raid were sunk, and the planned invasion force was repelled. From that point on, the offensive initiative swung to the Americans. The Japanese army and navy were irreversibly fated to operate on the defensive for the remainder of the war.

American land, sea, and air forces in the Pacific now began the slow but certain push into Japanese-occupied territory that would culminate in the assault on Japan itself. As they did so, the military's need for Japanese-speaking specialists grew accordingly. Japanese prisoners of war would have to be interrogated; radio and written communications from the Japanese military, once intercepted, would have to be translated, analyzed, and interpreted. Materials of all kinds, utterly impenetrable to American intelligence officers, would have to

Graduates of the Military Intelligence Service Language School broke codes and interpreted captured enemy documents, served on the front lines, and even worked as instructors. During the war, the school graduated about 6,000 Japanese-American linguists.

be sifted through and made of use to operations planners. The only way to accomplish this would be to bring into the service men with preexisting language skills or, at least, significant exposure to Japanese language and culture. The army, therefore, reversed its policy of excluding Japanese Americans and actively began to recruit them for training and duty with the Military Intelligence Service (MIS).

Headquartered at the Presidio in San Francisco, the MIS Language School was ordered to prepare Japanese-American specialists for immediate service in the Pacific theater with American forces stationed there. The fact that these future interrogators and translators were Japanese, and thus were excluded from the West Coast, even if in uniform, necessitated the transfer of the language training center from California to Camp Savage and later Fort Snelling in Minnesota. There, it was hoped, a corps of elite language experts would be readied to go to war.

Before this could happen, though, men had to be located and recruited voluntarily in the absence of a draft applicable

TRAINING TO TALK

The Military Intelligence Service Language School had the mission of training Japanese-American recruits to translate, interpret, and analyze documents, as well as interrogate Japanese prisoners of war. The school did not, however, enjoy the luxury of time. The army desperately needed translation services as larger amounts of captured intelligence materials accumulated and as Japanese prisoners began to trickle in. Men had to be prepared for duty and then immediately assigned to combat and intelligence units operating throughout the Pacific, if these sources of information were to be exploited in full. This one constraint meant that students at the school worked and studied incessantly in classrooms that had none of the technological aids taken for granted in modern language laboratories. All work was performed from textbooks and later practiced in lecture sessions often given by Kibei instructors with

to Japanese Americans. That search began in Hawaii but rapidly shifted to the War Relocation Authority centers, where the army anticipated finding a deep pool of Nisei and Kibei volunteers who, by virtue of their ethnic background alone, could be quickly and easily taught to question prisoners, translate radio intercepts, and read reams of captured documents. The army teams that went to find these men, however, failed to anticipate just how thoroughly American they would be. The Kibei, schooled in Japan, to be sure, possessed useful language skills and had extensive firsthand exposure to Japanese cultural traditions, but the Nisei had little, if any, of either. When interviewed by MIS personnel, only 3 percent of the Nisei candidates proved fluent in Japanese. The experience of one young prospect illustrates the language school's problem:

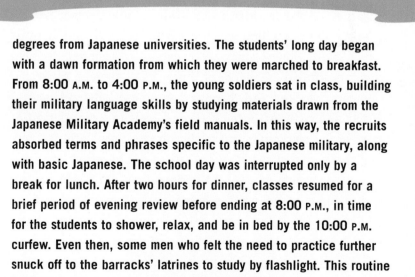

degrees from Japanese universities. The students' long day began with a dawn formation from which they were marched to breakfast. From 8:00 A.M. to 4:00 P.M., the young soldiers sat in class, building their military language skills by studying materials drawn from the Japanese Military Academy's field manuals. In this way, the recruits absorbed terms and phrases specific to the Japanese military, along with basic Japanese. The school day was interrupted only by a break for lunch. After two hours for dinner, classes resumed for a brief period of evening review before ending at 8:00 P.M., in time for the students to shower, relax, and be in bed by the 10:00 P.M. curfew. Even then, some men who felt the need to practice further snuck off to the barracks' latrines to study by flashlight. This routine held for every day of the week, with time off given only on Saturday afternoons and Sundays.

"I thought I [had] a fair speaking knowledge of the language," the potential recruit later recalled, "but [the interviewer] quickly proved me completely inadequate. . . . First he asked me to read a high school text. I could make out perhaps two or three characters in a hundred."[3]

Yet what they lacked in language skills, the Nisei who were eventually accepted by the MIS made up for in sheer determination and devotion to duty. The young men understood how important language services would be as the Pacific battlefields moved closer to Japan. Given that solid intelligence could mean the difference between victory and defeat, the MIS recruits worked diligently through 1942. A future translator studying at Camp Savage noted how Nisei drawn from Hawaii and the mainland, despite many differences, "were alike in our determination to do our best because thousands of American lives depended upon our ability to extract information from the enemy. . . . We were the eyes and ears for the American war effort."[4]

Of the 6,000 recruits who left Hawaii and the mainland relocation camps to attend the Military Intelligence Service school, 5,000 graduated and were attached to combat units in the Pacific. There, they were generally assigned to field teams in immediate need of linguists. Japanese-American MIS teams worked with captured Japanese battle plans and written orders, signal intercepts, and real-time translation of Japanese military radio and telegraph communications. Over time, their language skills were honed to the point at which Japanese prisoners of war under interrogation could not even identify their questioners as being Americans. "None of the Japanese prisoners," a former MIS sergeant wrote, "ever knew we were Japanese Americans." An officer this sergeant was interrogating in January 1945 even interrupted their session to assert confidently, "I'm positive you're from the Kansai area [of Japan]."[5] Oddly enough, the sergeant's parents came from precisely that region.

ONE PUKA PUKA

While the men of the MIS were at school in Minnesota, next door in Wisconsin, another group of Japanese Americans was training for actual combat. Although the government did not want to put young Nisei in uniform, some were already in the army when war broke out. After Pearl Harbor, the army was unsure what to do with Japanese Americans serving in its ranks, especially those in the Hawaii National Guard, the 298th and 299th Infantry Regiments. General John L. DeWitt urged their immediate reassignment to non-combat status as labor battalions. Assistant Secretary of War John J. McCloy, however, supported a proposal that the regiments be merged into a combat formation to be used in the Mediterranean area of operations against the Germans and Italians. His superior, Secretary of War Henry Stimson, saw a propaganda victory of the first order in the idea of a Japanese-American unit. "The effect," Stimson reasoned, "of the yellow man voluntarily fighting for the white would be substantial" in countering Japanese claims that American racism extended all the way to the battlefield.[6] General George Marshall, the army chief of staff, agreed, and in May 1942, he ordered the joining of the 298th and 299th into a new all-Japanese-American unit—the 100th Battalion (Separate).

Known to its members as the One Puka Puka ("One Zero Zero" in Hawaiian slang), the 100th was an over-strength battalion, having six companies rather than the normal contingent of four. For this reason, it functioned without being attached to a larger regiment and, hence, was considered "separate." Once assembled, the new formation was shipped quickly from Hawaii to the mainland for combat training. Arriving in Oakland, California, aboard the USS *Maui*, the 100th was less than impressive in appearance. One officer waiting to greet the Hawaiians described what he saw: "God, what a motley-looking crew. . . . They all needed a haircut. . . . Most of them didn't have their shoes laced. . . . They had their shirts out instead of inside their pants."[7] In this rather disheveled condition, the One Puka Puka boarded trains in Oakland bound for Camp McCoy in Wisconsin.

During their training, the men of the 100th learned the skills they would need to survive and win on the battlefields of North Africa, Italy, and later France. Throughout the early summer of 1942, the soldiers worked hard to turn themselves into some of the best troops in the U.S. Army. Their officers knew they had to succeed; the men accepted the fact that the cost of success might be their own lives: "We knew we had to shed blood. That was the price we're going to pay."[8] Fully trained by August, the 100th left Wisconsin for Morocco to participate in Operation Torch, the invasion of North Africa. This would be the first, but not the last place, where the 100th Battalion (Separate) would shed that blood.

A UNIT OF THEIR OWN

The 100th had been put together from existing army units made up of Hawaiian Nisei. The MIS, although hoping to rely upon mainland Nisei, was quickly filled with Kibei who had better language skills than their colleagues who had not studied in Japan. Frustrating as it was for the thousands of able-bodied young men languishing in the WRA internment camps, no American military unit had yet been formed that drew specifically on their reservoir of devotion and patriotism. Willing to serve their country at a moment's notice, many of these potential recruits bristled at the realization that their government was actively rejecting their service. Those who applied for but were refused acceptance to the MIS school were especially bitter. WRA chief Dillon Myer, on a tour of the Gila River camp, overheard a young Nisei comment to a friend how "nobody but a damned *Kibei* can get into this man's army."[9] Many internees, like this one, were ready to fight; none, as yet, had been asked.

Officials across the government agencies understood this and the opportunity that was being missed solely because of racism, suspicion, and fear. By late 1942, prominent government figures were calling for releases to be granted to Japanese-American internees of fighting age, so they could be inducted into the army. Franklin D. Roosevelt was well aware that many of his closet advisers were talking publicly about the formation of a new "Japanese Battalion," but the president insisted that any such unit be authorized only if "political advantages are to be gained."[10] Milton Eisenhower, now at the Office of War Information after leaving the WRA, held that one such advantage lay, as was the case with the 100th Battalion, in the raw propaganda value of putting Japanese Americans in uniform and on the battlefield. "Japanese propaganda," Eisenhower wrote in an October 1942 memo to Roosevelt, "insists that this is a racial war. We can combat this . . . only if our deeds permit us to tell the truth."[11] The first of these actions, Eisenhower claimed, would have to be the creation of a Japanese-American unit.

Still, others spoke in opposition. General DeWitt, for one, argued strongly against more Japanese Americans in the army. He had been a vocal opponent of allowing the 100th into combat and had only grudgingly accepted the need for Japanese in the MIS. The general viewed a new formation as an invitation to disaster. DeWitt saw only enemy faces among the internees and had long since convinced himself that "there are no persons of Japanese ancestry of 'unquestioned loyalty' in this country."[12] Like others, DeWitt urged Roosevelt to keep the Japanese where they were, but in the end Roosevelt disagreed. On February 1, 1943, the president announced, with some irony given the racial character of internment, that the "proposal to organize a combat team consisting of loyal American citizens of Japanese descent has my full approval. . . . Americanism is not, and never was, a matter of race or ancestry."[13]

THE 442ND TAKES SHAPE

Not having suffered the indignity of internment, Hawaiian Nisei leapt even more quickly than their mainland counterparts at the chance to volunteer for the new Japanese-American

The 442nd Regimental Combat Team was the first all-Nisei U.S. Army combat unit. The 442nd served with distinction, becoming the most highly decorated military unit for its size and length of service in the history of the U.S. Armed Forces, earning the nickname "The Purple Heart Battalion."

unit. In March 1943, 2,686 Nisei recruits from Hawaii sailed for Oakland with orders to proceed to Camp Shelby in Mississippi. The storm-tossed waters of the Pacific proved to be the first of many trials the new soldiers would endure. "Seasick! ... Life is miserable," one recruit wrote in his diary before jotting down that the "AJA [Americans of Japanese Ancestry] unit is to be called 442nd Infantry."[14]

The 100th Battalion had been shipped overseas by the time that the 442nd Regimental Combat Team came into existence. Unlike the One Puka Puka, the 442nd was composed not only of Hawaiian Nisei but also of mainland Nisei from the West Coast via the relocation centers. For this latter group of young men, the decision to volunteer had not come easily. The U.S. government had humiliated and interned them and still kept their loved ones behind barbed wire. It was, therefore, agonizingly difficult for some to put aside their anger at being held captive in their own country and volunteer to defend it. A volunteer from Topaz noted how incredulous people were at the very notion of his enlistment. His friends and family asked, "Why do you want to volunteer? ... You must have holes in your head."[15] Another remarked on the irony of a situation in which "parents had lost everything ... and here their sons were going to volunteer for the country that had disowned them."[16] One Issei father at the Rohwer camp resigned himself to his son's decision to join up, saying, "This is your country, so you do what you think is right. Whatever you do, don't bring shame to the family name."[17] Not everyone in the WRA camps, however, was as forgiving of what could be thought of as betrayal. A recruit from Tule Lake recalled how he showed up at the mess hall for dinner one night only to find a bone lying on his table. A note attached to the bone read, "Dogs eat here."[18]

Going for Broke
and Going Home

Despite the misgivings of their parents and the disdain of some of their comrades who felt nothing but hostility toward the government, men from each and every internment camp volunteered to serve in the new 442nd. Recruits came from Manzanar, Topaz, and Gila River. Poston camp, in Arizona, sent 236 of its Nisei boys to Camp Shelby by June 1943. Minidoka outdid that by contributing 308 men. Even the relatively tiny camps at Jerome and Rohwer gave 42 and 40 men, respectively. Together with the Hawaiians, these men began to train, and within a month, they felt enough esprit de corps (morale or group spirit) to give their regiment a motto: Go for Broke.

Yet it would take more than a stirring motto to weld two disparate groups of young Japanese Americans into a single, seamless fighting unit. Neither the Hawaiians nor the mainland Nisei really understood or fully accepted the other. The

Hawaiians were culturally more Asian in their customs and outlook and came from a place where they represented a majority of the population. The mainlanders had much in common with their white American neighbors and gave less cultural and social attention to things Japanese. They had endured hardships unknown to the Hawaiians, moreover, because of their minority status at home. Individually, mainland Nisei considered their Hawaiian brethren to be overly aggressive, crude, clannish, and ignorant; the Hawaiians thought of the mainlanders as weak, effeminate, too Americanized, aloof, and snobbish. Hawaiians called the West Coast Nisei "kotonks," for the sound their heads made when they hit the floor during any of the seemingly daily fights that broke out between the two sides. The mainlanders returned the favor by labeling the Hawaiians "Buddhaheads," a play on the Japanese word for "pig."

The arrival of experienced Japanese-American noncommissioned officers at Camp Shelby helped to alleviate some of the tension between the trainees. Most of the new sergeants had served in integrated units before Pearl Harbor and had little tolerance for petty rivalries that undermined unit morale. Perhaps an even more potent unifying force was the shared experience of racial prejudice that awaited any nonwhite in the then-segregated American South. An army report in 1943 detailed some of the difficulties faced by Nisei trainees in Mississippi: "House owners refusing to rent to Japanese . . . Caucasian girls declining to dance with Japanese-American soldiers at the USO . . . uncouth treatment of the Japanese Americans by some local M.P.s [military policemen]."[1]

The ultimate stamp of unity, however, was imprinted on the 442nd by a series of visits to the Jerome and Rohwer internment camps in Arkansas, organized by the regiment's commander, Colonel Charles W. Pence. Pence figured that part of the problem in unit cohesion between the Hawaiians and the mainlanders emerged out of the disparity in the groups' treatment at the hands of the government. The colonel reasoned

On June 21, 2000, Senator Daniel K. Inouye (D-Hawaii) was one of 22 Asian-American soldiers that received the Medal of Honor for service in World War II. Despite multiple wounds, Inouye, first lieutenant of the 442nd Regimental Combat Team, crawled up a hill and used grenades and a submachine gun to knock out three German machine-gun nests, near Terenzo, Italy, on April 20, 1945.

that a visit by the Hawaiian Nisei to a relocation center might allow them a glimpse into the lives of their mainland comrades and an appreciation for what the West Coast Nisei had been and were still experiencing. Pence's plan worked splendidly. After touring the camp at Rohwer, the Hawaiians gained a new respect for the obstacles their fellow Japanese Americans had overcome. "It was mind-boggling," wrote the soldier and future U.S. senator Daniel Inouye. "The thing that went through my mind constantly was: 'I wonder what I would have done. Would I have volunteered?' . . . We weren't herded away. But these guys [the West Coast Nisei] were herded into camps like this, and they volunteered."[2] Another Hawaiian suddenly realized a new kinship and expressed it in blunt terms: "I was p— off for the relocation guys."[3]

A new sense of camaraderie sprang up among the men of the 442nd. Along with it came a fighting spirit that was in many ways unique. The men of the combat team, first and foremost, knew that they would be struggling to re-establish liberty in Europe, while combating the denial of it for their families at home. Both battles would be hard, and both would be heroic. Their training at Camp Shelby, however, only focused on the task at hand—defeating America's enemies in the mountains and valleys of Italy. There, a German enemy stood ready to offer the 442nd the first of many tests it would face under fire.

RESISTANCE AT HEART MOUNTAIN

As the 442nd trained for war in Europe, it became clear to the Roosevelt administration that another ready source of military manpower laid unexploited within the confines of the War Relocation Authority centers. The response to the call for volunteers in 1942 and 1943 had been so positive that the government lifted the ban on drafting Japanese Americans and extended the Selective Service to the internment camps, fully expecting a wave of eager and willing draftees to roll out of the centers. Reality proved to be somewhat more complex. Until January 1944, those Japanese-American men who signed up for the military—and women who signed up for auxiliary service—did so freely. Those who refused to endanger their lives for a nation that had stripped them of their dignity, security, and constitutional rights were similarly free to reject military service.

Roosevelt's extension of the draft, however, replaced volunteerism with legalized coercion. Japanese Americans who resented federal power and its misuse in relocating them now would be forced by law to serve the government's interests. The prospect of induction infuriated otherwise patriotic men who felt that they owed the U.S. government nothing. Resistance to the draft thus rose swiftly at all of the WRA camps and most publicly at Heart Mountain.

Isolated in the vast open expanses of Wyoming, Heart Mountain became the headquarters of the Fair Play Committee, a group of Japanese-American internees determined to ignore the government's demand for draftees. When ordered to present themselves for the routine army physical examinations, the Fair Play members refused to appear. In a written protest, they declared:

> We the Nisei have been complacent and too inarticulate to the unconstitutional acts that we were subjected to. If ever there was a time or cause for decisive action, IT IS NOW! . . . 110,000 innocent people were kicked out of their homes . . . and herded like dangerous criminals into concentration camps with barbed-wire fences. . . . We members of the Fair Play Committee hereby refuse to go to the physical examination or to the induction if or when we are called.[4]

The Fair Play Committee resisters were determined not to sacrifice anything for a national government that had wrongly imprisoned them and their loved ones. As one put it, they refused to be drafted meekly and "sheep-like into segregated combat units [and] become cannon fodder to gain acceptance by the Great White Father [in Washington, D.C.]."[5] In the course of the protests, the committee asked for little outside support and received very little in return. The ACLU, approached by the Fair Play leadership regarding legal assistance, advised the organization to abandon any hope of victory in the courtroom.

Those men who refused to be inducted, the ACLU reported, certainly had that right but should expect jail time if it were exercised. Fair Play members "who counseled others to resist," on the other hand, were "not within their rights and must expect severe treatment, whatever justifications they feel."[6] Even Minoru Yasui, who had pressed his own case against the government, mocked the Heart Mountain resisters as "sullen and resentful [in whom] traces of self-pity can be discerned."[7]

Thus on their own, the Fair Play men struggled onward. In May 1944, 63 members refused to appear for mandatory physicals and were arrested. Facing a judge in Wyoming's largest mass trial, all were convicted of resisting the draft; each received a three-year prison sentence. The group's seven-member leadership council was soon indicted by a grand jury and convicted of counseling others to avoid conscription. All of the Fair Play leaders received terms of four years behind bars. After serving 18 months, however, their sentences were overturned on appeal.

The convictions at Heart Mountain broke the effort there, but did not end the anti-draft movement at the other camps. At Tule Lake, 27 men fought induction and, in this instance, won the right not to serve. The presiding judge ruled that none had to make themselves liable to the draft, concluding that "it is shocking to the conscience [that imprisoned men] under duress and restraint be compelled to serve in the armed forces" of the country that was incarcerating them without due process.[8] Resisters at Poston camp were convicted in their trials, but a similarly sympathetic Arizona judge sentenced them to no prison time and a fine of only one cent each. A further 315 Japanese-American men would resist induction by the time the internment program ended.

THE 442ND GOES TO WAR

The men of the Fair Play Committee were battling injustice at Heart Mountain just as the 442nd Regimental Combat

Team, true to its motto, was preparing to go for broke in Italy. Meanwhile, the 100th Battalion, which had already seen heavy action in North Africa, landed with the Allied invasion force at Salerno, Italy, in September 1943. Casualties in the 100th soon climbed high enough to earn it the nickname "The Purple Heart Battalion."[9] Together with the rest of the U.S. 5th Army, the 100th had the unenviable assignment of pushing inland and northward against stiffening German resistance toward Rome, in the process breaching the German defenses along the heavily fortified Gustav Line that stretched nearly the width of the Italian peninsula.

The American divisions that came ashore at Salerno, soon joined by those of the British 8th Army pushing up from the toe of Italy, quickly became bogged down in some of the most ferocious fighting of World War II. The Germans contested every inch of rocky Italian ground along the Gustav Line, determined to bleed the Allies dry and halt their gains in the Mediterranean. After months of bitter combat during the summer and fall of 1943, it became painfully obvious to Allied planners that the German defenses could not be breached by frontal assault. Consequently, Operation Shingle was launched in January 1944.

Designed to break the Gustav Line by going around it, the operation involved an amphibious landing at Anzio that was to spearhead a lightning strike toward Rome. Just the opposite occurred. The landing force experienced fierce German counterattacks, led by armored units, nearly from the moment it waded ashore. It took five months for the U.S. VII Corps to break out of the Anzio bridgehead. The 100th Battalion, like the other American units at Anzio, suffered greatly and was significantly weakened when it was joined by the 442nd in June 1944, just before the VII Corps captured Rome. Two months later, the Japanese-American formations were officially redesignated as a single fighting force, the 100th Battalion/442nd Regimental Combat Team.

After the 442nd Combat Team famously rescued 230 men from the Lost Battalion, an infantry that was surrounded by German forces in the Vosges mountains, they fought alongside segregated troops of the British and French empires and the non-segregated Brazilian Expeditionary Force, which had in its ranks ethnic Japanese. Pictured, infantrymen from the 442nd regiment run for cover inside a building as they are targeted by German artillery on the Italian front.

On to France

Two days after the liberation of Rome, Allied divisions stormed ashore in Normandy. Operation Overlord, the invasion of France, had begun. Planned as a two-part operation, the assault on what the German leader Adolf Hitler had called Fortress Europe had northern and southern strategic components. The Normandy landings in the north were to be supported by similar ones in southern France codenamed Operation Dragoon and scheduled for August 15, 1944. Although the main body of the 100th/442nd remained in Italy as Dragoon commenced, the unit's anti-tank company went ashore with the invasion force and was soon joined by the rest of the regiment. While the Normandy force advanced northeastward from the

A DIFFERENT KIND OF CAMP

The West Coast Nisei soldiers who served in the 442nd had experienced life behind barbed wire. Recruited from the War Relocation Authority camps at the height of their operation, the men knew the humiliation and degradation of being imprisoned, not for what they had done but because they were part of a stigmatized social minority. Yet for all they had known at places like Manzanar and Topaz, the members of the 442nd who helped liberate the inmates of the infamous Nazi concentration camp at Dachau had never witnessed the ultimate expression of racist hatred. Japanese Americans had been locked away in desolate outposts, but they never suffered torments even remotely resembling those endured by Jews and others deemed by the Nazis to be unworthy of life. The soldiers of the 522nd Field Artillery saw firsthand what happened when the same fear and hate that drove their own government's internment program devolved into torture and murder. Following are two soldiers' accounts of what the 522nd found as it arrived at Dachau in April 1945:

English Channel, the Dragoon armies marched northward, sending the German Army Group G rceling before them. By the fall of 1944, Army Group G had merged with Army Group B, which had been retreating from Normandy, to form a new German defensive line anchored in the south by positions in the Vosges Mountains of France. Here, the Japanese-American soldiers of the 442nd would face their toughest test.

The fighting in the mountains became more intense as the autumn chill set in, in October 1944, with both sides hoping

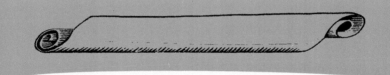

As we approached . . . the snow-covered fields of Dachau . . . we unexpectedly witnessed a most gruesome and pitiful sight: hundreds upon hundreds of emaciated, gaunt, malnourished people in black-and-white prison clothing. Their eyes were sunken and their cheeks hollow. They were living skeletons, wandering aimlessly about the countryside.*

We came to a real peaceful-looking town. It was called Dachau. . . . Right in the middle of town was what looked like a big factory with a high fence all around and two big brick smokestacks in the middle. Before we ever reached it we noticed the odd smell. . . . The smell of decaying human flesh. There were dead corpses all piled up everywhere in there. . . . I was very shook up. I kept trying to figure out what the heck is this doggone thing?**

* *Japanese Eyes, American Heart: Personal Reflections of Hawaii's World War II Nisei Soldiers*, compiled by the Hawaii Nikkei History Editorial Board. Honolulu: University of Hawaii Press, 2000, p. 286.
** Inada, p. 381.

to gain the advantage before winter. Here and there, American units broke through the German defenses only to fall back in the face of stiff resistance or, in the case of the famous Lost Battalion rescued by the 442nd, to find themselves cut off behind enemy lines. On October 27, the 442nd received news that a contingent of men had been surrounded by German troops on one of a series of low hills near their position. The regiment was ordered "to break through the reinforced German line of resistance and relieve the 1st Battalion, 141st Infantry."[10] Trapped in enemy territory, 211 American soldiers clung to their position despite intense German machine gun and mortar fire. In the meantime, the troops of the 442nd fought their way toward the encircled G.I.s through forests thick with German patrols and machine-gun nests, enduring days and nights punctuated by artillery barrages. Finally, on October 30, the Japanese Americans reached their beleaguered comrades in the Lost Battalion after combat that cost the 442nd 60 percent of its strength in casualties. The commander of the besieged unit, Second Lieutenant Marty Higgins, summed up the feelings of his men when he radioed his divisional headquarters to report the arrival of the Nisei soldiers: "442 here. Tell them we love them."[11]

After the Vosges campaign, the 442nd was transferred back to Italy, and there won further laurels in the last days of fighting along the last of the great German defensive bulwarks, or barriers, of World War II, the Gothic Line. Only one element of the 442nd was left behind to continue the war in France, the 522nd Field Artillery Battalion. These men were some of the first Americans to encounter the horrors of the Nazi regime in Germany when they liberated a satellite facility of the concentration camp at Dachau, near Munich, in early 1945. The irony of freeing inmates of a concentration camp in Germany while their own families were still sitting in American internment camps did not escape the men and brought into sharp relief the injustices that had been inflicted on Japanese Americans. News of the feats of the 100th/442nd in Europe and the sight of

Japanese-American soldiers liberating Nazi camp victims galvanized support within the U.S. government for the establishment of a release and resettlement program that would close the relocation centers and allow the internees to go home.

GOING HOME

In July 1944, just weeks before the 442nd went into combat in France, the new Western Defense Commander, General Charles H. Bonesteel, informed President Roosevelt that, in the army's opinion, there was no further need for the internment of Japanese Americans. Already, the Jerome camp had been shut and, primarily through work releases, some 23,000 Japanese Americans had been resettled in the Midwest and on the East Coast. More than 1,000 had returned to the exclusion zone. In cities such as Chicago, Denver, and New York, some former internees were rebuilding their lives as free citizens by the summer of 1944. "Reception everywhere has been most heartening," one of these fortunate individuals wrote back in a letter to an internment camp newspaper after release.[12] Cincinnati, another reported, was "a good place for evacuees to relocate in. . . . There are some 100 job offerings waiting to be accepted now."[13]

Bonesteel took such correspondences as a sign that release was feasible and, in any case, warranted by Japan's imminent defeat and the evaporation of any possible threat to the West Coast. President Roosevelt and many people in California, however, remained skeptical. Roosevelt, for his part, preferred to wait until after the presidential election of 1944 to decide on a comprehensive camp closure and return plan. He feared a backlash at the polls if he moved too quickly. His secretary of the interior, Harold Ickes, wrote at the time that it was "the president himself who has insisted that the ban [on Japanese Americans] not be lifted until after the election."[14]

Roosevelt's apprehensions were seemingly confirmed by army reports from California stating "that the majority opinion in all of the area . . . was decidedly against the return of

Japanese."[15] Roosevelt's victory in November 1944, however, allowed him to proceed with the closing of the internment camps as advised. One of the first steps along this path came on January 2, 1945, with the rescinding of General John DeWitt's West Coast exclusion order, allowing for the return of all Japanese Americans except those who still held a "pro-Japanese attitude."[16] Since the war with Japan continued to rage in the Pacific, the government had no intention of releasing anyone who had been judged disloyal or had requested to renounce their American citizenship, as some Nisei had done. Issei who had asked to be repatriated to Japan after the war were similarly excluded from any proposed release program. This group included some 7,000 of the 18,000 people interned at Tule Lake, 65 percent of whom were American-born Nisei. In total, 5,766 Nisei renounced their citizenship during internment, and of these, 4,724 eventually would be sent to Japan from WRA relocation centers. Unlike their Issei elders, sailing for Japan would not be a homecoming for the Nisei who chose to leave America. Their motivations were varied, but most would have agreed with one young man who refused to wait for the situation "to get better in this country for minority groups" and said that at least in Japan, he would "look like everyone else."[17]

Yet while a minority of men and women were preparing for a new life in Japan, most internees were getting ready to go home. After the January order ending exclusion, nearly 70,000 Japanese Americans were released by the WRA, two-thirds of whom returned to the West Coast, 43,581 to California alone. As the camps began to close, their inmates were provided with money—$25 for individuals, $50 for families—and train tickets to their former residences or any other destination of their choice. For many of the 1,862 internees who died behind barbed wire, return meant reburial. For the 5,918 Japanese-American babies born in the camps, release was truly a new beginning.

Going back to the lives they led before Pearl Harbor, however, was neither an easy nor an altogether safe proposition. The

In February 1985, the Manzanar internment camp was designated a National Historic Landmark. Once a prison for Japanese Americans during World War II, today the site has been visited by more than half a million people on guided tours. Pictured are the remains of Manzanar's front gate with the Sierra Nevada Mountains in the background.

WRA reported in May 1945 that in California "24 incidents of violence or open intimidation have been recorded—15 shooting attacks, one attempted dynamiting, three arson cases, and five threatening visits."[18] Across the West, returning Japanese Americans were sent the brutal message that, as a defense lawyer for a group of white arsonists proudly proclaimed, "This is a white man's country."[19] Even veterans, fresh from the battlefields of Europe, were subjected to discrimination and harassment, although here tempered by the fact of their proud service to the country. One severely wounded and disabled 442nd veteran, for example, recalled a day when his war injuries prevented him from filling his car's fuel tank and how the gas station owner confessed, "I had signs on my service station saying 'No Jap Trade Wanted.' . . . Now when I see you come back like that, I feel so small."[20]

Of the 10 WRA relocation centers that opened in 1942, 8 closed in October and November 1945. One, Jerome, had been shut down in 1944, and another, the notorious segregation center at Tule Lake, remained in operation until March 20, 1946. With its closure, the camp experience physically ended for Japanese Americans; it ended politically with President Harry S. Truman's Executive Order 9742, which terminated the WRA and its mission on June 30, 1946. The emotional and psychological experience of being unjustly imprisoned by one's own government, though, would linger in the memories of the former internees for the rest of their days.

Who Is an American? The Legacy of Japanese-American Internment

President Franklin Delano Roosevelt's relationship with the people he interned was characterized by public ambivalence and private hostility toward the very notion that they could be considered wholly American. The same president who signed Executive Order 9066 in February 1942 could turn around and officially deny the relevance of race when creating the 442nd Regimental Combat Team nearly a year later. In his capacity as president, Roosevelt proudly declared that every American could lay claim to the rights of justice and equality protected in the Constitution, without regard to skin color or ancestry. Yet behind the closed doors of the White House, Roosevelt shared the racist attitudes that pervaded white America in the 1940s. The president never shied away from using slurs in ordinary conversation and often mused over the racial differences that separated Japanese Americans from their white countrymen and the supposed inferiority of Japanese culture when compared with that of Europe. Roosevelt cynically put his re-election bid in 1944 ahead of any moral commitment to end the relocation program and, just before his sudden death in April 1945, demonstrated a callous lack of remorse for the human suffering caused by his 1942 internment order. When Roosevelt received a copy of Ansel Adams's photographic catalog of the Japanese-American internment experience, a book entitled *Born Free and Equal*, he refused to open the book, let alone study the pictures depicting life behind the fences of his government's camps.

Roosevelt's failure to acknowledge the injustice of forcibly relocating loyal Americans was all the more obvious in light of the process of redress and reparation initiated by his successor, Harry S. Truman. Famous for his 1948 order desegregating the U.S. armed forces, Truman also made it a point to begin to heal the national wound opened in 1942. It was Truman who definitively and proudly cast the internment program into history's dustbin by signing Executive Order 9742, terminating the WRA and its mission. Similarly, it was Truman who personally awarded the Presidential Unit Citation in 1948 to the 442nd saying, "You have fought against prejudice and you have won."[1]

That same year, undoubtedly following the president's lead, Congress passed the Japanese-American Claims Act, allocating $38 million for the settlement of property claims arising out of internment. Eventually, more than 23,000 claimants received compensation for losses suffered as a result of involuntary evacuation and relocation. The Senate report on the act stated that the question of whether the relocation was justified was "now moot. The government did move these people, bodily, the resulting loss was great, and the principles of justice and responsible government requires that there should be compensation for such losses."[2] The final disbursement of funds provided for in the 1948 legislation came in 1965.

In 1999, the U.S. Justice Department agreed to a $1.6 billion reparations program for Japanese Americans interned during World War II and settled with 181 ethnic Japanese from Latin America who suffered similar treatment. Pictured is Alicia Nishimoto, a Latin Japanese American from Peru who was interned in the United States during the war.

Throughout the 1950s, as the country struggled with the paranoia generated by the hunt for suspected Communists, a new awareness developed among Americans regarding the assault on core national values represented by the internment program. The significance of defining who was and in what was an American became apparent as political extremists sowed fear and suspicion across the country. The cultural and racial awakening that took place during the tumultuous 1960s and early 1970s further sensitized people to the consequences of denying loyal citizens the label of American and the necessity of paying the debt owed to more than 100,000 men, women, and children who experienced just such a denial. Given this new atmosphere of reconciliation, it is not surprising that in 1976 Gerald Ford became the first American president to declare that the internment program had been not only a grave

AN AMERICAN PROMISE

In 1976, President Gerald Ford promised Japanese Americans and the nation that no loyal citizen would ever again pay for their ancestry with their freedom. The president did so in a proclamation, excerpts of which are presented here, made during celebrations marking the 200th birthday of the United States:

> In this bicentennial year, we are commemorating the anniversary dates of many great events in American history. An honest reckoning, however, must include a recognition of our national mistakes as well as our national achievements. . . . February 19th is the anniversary of a sad day in American history. It was on that date in 1942, . . . that Executive Order 9066 was issued . . . [and more than] 100,000 persons of Japanese ancestry were removed from their homes, detained in special camps, and eventually relocated. . . . We now know what we should have known then—not only was that evacuation wrong, but Japanese Americans were and are loyal Americans. . . . I think it appropriate, in this our bicentennial year, to remove all doubt on that matter, and to make clear our commitment to the future. . . . I call upon the American people to affirm with me this American promise—that we have learned from the tragedy of that long-ago experience forever to treasure liberty and justice for each individual American, and resolve that this kind of action shall never again be repeated.*

* Inada, p. 410–411.

injustice but also a violation of civil liberties that should have been recognized as an unpardonable error even during a time of national crisis.

The pressures of war, in other words, offered little by way of an excuse for incarcerating innocent citizens merely because of their racial heritage. The next occupant of the White House, Jimmy Carter, took Ford's honest insight and contrition and used its moral force to generate support for comprehensive legislation aimed at providing reparation payments to survivors of the internment camps and thus fully re-establishing their status as Americans.

THE CIVIL LIBERTIES ACT OF 1988

Under President Carter, the Commission on the Wartime Relocation and Internment of Civilians was set to work in 1980. The commission's assignment was to study the events that led to and followed from Executive Order 9066 and to recommend an appropriate form of government compensation. To collect the needed data, the commission held public hearings in San Francisco, Los Angeles, Seattle, New York, and Chicago and heard testimony from key government figures including John J. McCloy, Edward Ennis, and Karl Bendetsen. After extensive investigation, the commission issued its findings and recommendations in June 1983. The panel advised Congress and the administration of then-President Ronald Reagan to offer a formal apology to those who had suffered under the internment program, issue pardons to Fred Korematsu and the others convicted of violating the wartime West Coast exclusion orders, restore any federal entitlements lost as a result of evacuation, compensate camp survivors, and establish a fund for an internment education program.

Five years later, Congress began consideration of the Civil Liberties Act of 1988, a piece of legislation designed by its sponsors specifically to fulfill the recommendation of the commission. During the debate over the measure in the House, Representative Norman Mineta, a former Heart Mountain internee, addressed his colleagues: "We are not talking here about the wartime sacrifices that we all made to support and defend our nation. At issue here is the wholesale violation, based on race, of those very legal principles we were fighting to defend."[3] Mineta urged his fellow lawmakers to complete America's collective act of contrition by passing the Civil Liberties Act. They did, and the bill became law on August 10, 1988. A year later, in November 1989, President George H.W. Bush signed the Civil Liberties Act appropriations bill, which set aside $500 million a year until all former internees had been paid for their ordeal. With that, the U.S. government had officially settled the issue of Japanese-American loyalty by admitting Franklin Roosevelt's mistake and by paying to correct it. For citizens of Japanese ancestry, the question of who was an American had been answered at long last.

NEW FEARS, NEW CHALLENGES

Not long after the reparations payments had begun to be disbursed to former internees, the United States went to war in the Persian Gulf. Americans at home discovered a new minority group to fear—Arab Americans. As Japanese Americans were receiving apologies and reparations checks for the injustices done to them, "some government agencies," according to the historian Roger Daniels, "were acting as if the Arab-American minority in the United States was somehow allied with the Iraqi tyrant Saddam Hussein."[4] While no one at the time advocated any sort of mass detention of Arab Americans, some commentators and public figures did call for increased surveillance of individuals and groups suspected of disloyalty. Here and there across the nation, racist epithets and sporadic acts of violence, reminiscent of the 1940s, targeted a community many felt might be in league with a foreign enemy. The 1995 bombing of the World Trade Center in New York by Islamic extremists led even more people to cast a suspicious eye on their Arab neighbors. The September 11, 2001, terror-

Many Japanese Americans have seen parallels between the Japanese-American internment and the treatment of Arab Americans after the September 11 attacks. They question whether the historical lessons of World War II have been forgotten as post-9/11 programs have required men from mostly Arab and Muslim countries to register with the government and others have faced deportation. Above, women protest the registration program in New York City in 2003.

ist attack on the same buildings generated outright anti-Arab sentiment that in some cases bordered on hysterical. Assaults on Arab Americans, and anyone who looked like them, rose dramatically, as did calls for curtailing the civil liberties of anyone accused of terrorist acts or harboring sympathy for extremist causes. In response, more thoughtful Americans immediately cited the Japanese-American experience as a cautionary tale, warning the nation against any rush to judgment based on senseless stereotypes and ethnic prejudice. These observers admonished those who demanded that a harsh line be taken regarding Arab Americans to remember how, in the past, loyal Americans had been persecuted for nothing more than having a shared ancestry with the country's enemies.

Thus, as unjust and inhuman as the internment of Japanese Americans during World War II had been, it left a legacy of restraint that has and most likely will continue to act as a brake on government power and public outrage during times of national emergency. Future global events could very well create an atmosphere in which paranoia and racial hatred might once again flourish and lead to the persecution of any number of minority groups, as it had in 1942. The question of who is an American might once more lock innocent citizens behind camp gates. At that point, memories of places like Manzanar, Poston, and Heart Mountain could serve as keys to unlock those gates.

CHRONOLOGY

1882   The United States Congress passes the Chinese Exclusion Act, leading to an increase in Japanese immigration.

1906   San Francisco's board of education orders Japanese children to attend Chinese schools; strenuous protests by the Japanese government lead to the order's withdrawal and an agreement to limit future Japanese immigration.

1913   California passes a law prohibiting land purchases by Japanese farmers.

1922   The United States Supreme Court rules that Japanese immigrants cannot become naturalized citizens.

1924   The Immigration Act of 1924 effectively prohibits any further immigration from Japan.

1941   **December 8** The United States and Japan go to war after the Japanese attack on Pearl Harbor the previous day; detention of Japanese aliens begins.

1942   **February 19** President Franklin Delano Roosevelt signs Executive Order 9066 allowing for the evacuation and internment of all Japanese Americans living on the West Coast of the United States.

February 25 The first Japanese families are ordered to leave their homes.

March 2 Lieutenant General John L. DeWitt issues Public Proclamation No. 1, establishing two military areas in the West from which Japanese Americans would be excluded.

March 19 Congress passes Public Law 503 to provide penalties for violation of Executive Order 9066 and DeWitt's public proclamation.

March 27 General DeWitt puts Japanese Americans under an 8:00 P.M. to 6:00 A.M. curfew; registration begins for evacuation to assembly centers and, from there, to the newly opened internment camps.

March 28 Minoru Yasui violates DeWitt's curfew, becoming the first Japanese American to challenge the government's restrictions.

May 16 Gordon Hirabayashi refuses to register for evacuation and takes his case to court.

TIMELINE

December 8, 1941
The U.S. and Japan go to war after the attack on Pearl Harbor the previous day

March 2, 1942
Two military areas in the West, from which Japanese Americans would be excluded, are established

1941 ———————————————— **1943**

February 19, 1942
President Roosevelt signs Executive Order 9066

February 1, 1943
President Roosevelt authorizes the formation of the 442nd Regimental Combat Team

March 27, 1942
Registration begins for evacuation to assembly centers and, from there, to internment camps

May 30 Fred Korematsu is arrested in San Leandro, California, and charged with violating the government's exclusion order.

June 1 The newly relocated Military Intelligence Service Language School opens at Camp Savage, Minnesota.

July 13 Mitsuye Endo files a writ of habeas corpus and demands to be released from the Tanforan assembly center south of San Francisco.

1943   **February 1** President Roosevelt authorizes the formation of the 442nd Regimental Combat Team; the unit is later combined with the 100th Battalion (Separate), an all-Japanese-American unit in the U.S. Army.

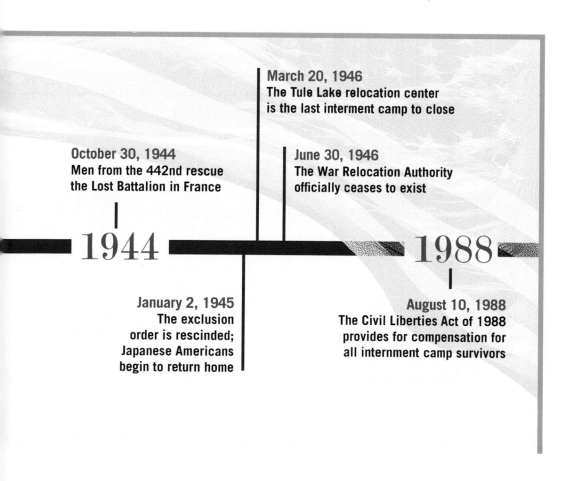

March 20, 1946
The Tule Lake relocation center
is the last interment camp to close

October 30, 1944
Men from the 442nd rescue
the Lost Battalion in France

June 30, 1946
The War Relocation Authority
officially ceases to exist

1944

1988

January 2, 1945
The exclusion
order is rescinded;
Japanese Americans
begin to return home

August 10, 1988
The Civil Liberties Act of 1988
provides for compensation for
all internment camp survivors

June 21 The Supreme Court rules against Gordon Hirabayashi and Minoru Yasui.

1944 **June 2** The 442nd arrives in Italy.

June 30 The relocation camp at Jerome, Arkansas, is the first to close; internees are transferred to other camps.

October 30 Men from the 442nd rescue the Lost Battalion in the Vosges Mountains in France.

December 18 *Korematsu v. United States* is settled in favor of the government; the internment policy is upheld; the *Endo* case is settled in favor of Mitsuye Endo's demand for habeas corpus.

1945 **January 2** DeWitt's exclusion order is rescinded; Japanese Americans begin to return home.

September 2 Japans surrenders; World War II ends.

1946 **March 20** The Tule Lake relocation center is the last interment camp to close.

June 30 The WRA officially ceases to exist.

1948 **July 2** Congress passes the Japanese-American Claims Act, beginning the process of reparation for internment.

1988 **August 10** The Civil Liberties Act of 1988 provides for compensation for all internment camp survivors.

NOTES

CHAPTER 1

1. Henry Berry, *"This is No Drill!"—Living Memories of the Attack on Pearl Harbor.* New York: Berkley Books, 1992, 69.
2. Ibid., 132.
3. Peter Irons, *Justice at War: The Story of the Japanese American Internment Cases.* Berkeley, Calif.: University of California Press, 1983, 6.
4. Burt Takeuchi, "Pearl Harbor: Asian Americans Witness Air Raid on December 7th, 1941," online at http://us_asians.tripod.com/articles-nihonmachi-outreach.html, 12/02/2008, 2.
5. Ibid., 3.
6. Lawson Fusao Inada, ed., *Only What We Could Carry: The Japanese American Internment Experience.* Berkeley, Calif.: Heyday Books, 2000, 31–32.
7. Takeuchi, "Pearl Harbor," 2.
8. Thomas G. Paterson, ed., *Major Problems in American Foreign Policy, Volume II: Since 1914.* New York: D.C. Heath and Company, 1989,189.
9. Irons, *Justice at War,* 19.
10. Ibid., 9.
11. Ibid., 6.
12. Ibid.
13. Inada, *Only What We Could Carry,* 14–15.

CHAPTER 2

1. Ronald Takaki, *A Different Mirror: A History of Multicultural America.* Boston: Little, Brown and Company, 1993, 192.
2. Irons, *Justice at War,* 9.
3. Takaki, *Different Mirror,* 246.
4. Ibid., 247.
5. Irons, *Justice at War,* 9.
6. Roger Daniels, *Prisoners Without Trial: Japanese Americans in World War II.* New York: Hill and Wang, 1993, 10.
7. Takaki, *Different Mirror,* 252.
8. Daniels, *Prisoners Without Trial,* 12.
9. Irons, *Justice at War,* 13.
10. Takaki, *Different Mirror,* 270.
11. Ibid., 270.
12. Ibid., 264.
13. Greg Robinson, *By Order of the President: FDR and the Internment of Japanese Americans.* Cambridge, Mass.: Harvard University Press, 2003, 31.
14. Ibid., 40–41.
15. Takaki, *Different Mirror,* 273.
16. Irons, *Justice at War,* 19.
17. Tetsuden Kashima, introduction to *Life Behind Barbed Wire: The World War II Internment Memoir of a Hawai'i Issei* by Yasutaro Soga. Honolulu: University of Hawaii Press, 2008, 2.

18. Takaki, *Different Mirror*, 275–276.
19. Irons, *Justice at War*, 22.
20. Robinson, *By Order of the President*, 69.
21. Daniels, *Prisoners Without Trial*, 25.

CHAPTER 3

1. Inada, *Only What We Could Carry*, 155.
2. Ibid., 58.
3. Ibid., 186.
4. Irons, *Justice at War*, 26.
5. Ibid., 30.
6. Ibid., 7.
7. Daniels, *Prisoners Without Trial*, 43.
8. Robinson, *By Order of the President*, 91.
9. Ibid.
10. Irons, *Justice at War*, 7.
11. Ibid., 41.
12. Ibid., 37.
13. Ibid., 52.
14. Robinson, *By Order of the President*, 96.
15. Irons, *Justice at War*, 53.
16. Robinson, *By Order of the President*, 99.
17. Irons, *Justice at War*, 28.
18. Ibid., 49.
19. Ibid., 47.
20. Robinson, *By Order of the President*, 105.
21. Irons, *Justice at War*, 57.
22. Ibid., 61.
23. Robinson, *By Order of the President*, 108.
24. Irons, *Justice at War*, 64.

CHAPTER 4

1. Robinson, *By Order of the President*, 148.
2. Ibid., 148.
3. Ibid., 150.
4. Ibid.
5. Ibid., 127.
6. Daniels, *Prisoners Without Trial*, 50.
7. Irons, *Justice at War*, 80.
8. Robinson, *By Order of the President*, 160.
9. Ibid., 142.
10. Irons, *Justice at War*, 65.
11. Ibid., 67.
12. Daniels, *Prisoners Without Trial*, 53.
13. Ibid., 55.
14. Inada, *Only What We Could Carry*, 71.
15. Ibid., 88.

CHAPTER 5

1. Irons, *Justice at War*, 71.
2. Daniels, *Prisoners Without Trial*, 57.
3. Ibid., 57.
4. Irons, *Justice at War*, 71.
5. Inada, *Only What We Could Carry*, 162–163.
6. Ibid., 104.
7. Ibid., 105.
8. Ibid., 93.
9. Irons, *Justice at War*, 74.
10. "War Relocation Authority Application for Leave Clearance," July 1942, online at www.cwu.edu/~geograph/faculty/lillquist_files/pubs/ja_relocation/appendixCloyaltyquestionnaire.pdf, 25 March 2009.

11. Inada, *Only What We Could Carry*, 121–122.
12. Robinson, *By Order of the President*, 200.
13. Ibid., 200.

CHAPTER 6

1. Irons, *Justice at War*, 81.
2. Ibid., 84.
3. Ibid., 88.
4. Ibid., 94.
5. Ibid., 102.
6. Ibid., 244.
7. Daniels, *Prisoners Without Trial*, 73.
8. Ibid., 74.
9. Inada, *Only What We Could Carry*, 281.
10. Daniels, *Prisoners Without Trial*, 75.
11. Inada, *Only What We Could Carry*, 265.
12. Ibid.
13. Robinson, *By Order of the President*, 190.
14. Ibid., 193.
15. Ibid., 203.
16. Ibid., 207.

CHAPTER 7

1. Inada, *Only What We Could Carry*, 14.
2. Ibid., 20.
3. Daniels, *Prisoners Without Trial*, 76.
4. *Japanese Eyes, American Heart: Personal Reflections of Hawaii's World War II Nisei Soldiers*, compiled by the Hawaii Nikkei History Editorial Board (Honolulu: University of Hawaii Press, 2000), 127.

5. Inada, *Only What We Could Carry*, 358.
6. Robinson, *By Order of the President*, 166.
7. Robert Asahina, *Just Americans: How Japanese Americans Won a War at Home and Abroad: The Story of the 100th Battalion/442nd Regimental Combat Team in World War II*. New York: Gotham Books, 2006, 33.
8. Asahina, *Just Americans*, 35.
9. Ibid., 44.
10. Robinson, *By Order of the President*, 168.
11. Ibid., 163.
12. Asahina, *Just Americans*, 49.
13. Ibid., 43.
14. *Japanese Eyes*, 53.
15. Asahina, *Just Americans*, 51.
16. Ibid.
17. Asahina, *Just Americans*, 52.
18. Ibid., 56.

CHAPTER 8

1. Asahina, *Just Americans*, 57.
2. Ibid., 63.
3. Ibid.
4. Inada, *Only What We Could Carry*, 409.
5. Ibid., 314.
6. Ibid., 318.
7. Irons, *Justice at War*, 87.
8. Inada, *Only What We Could Carry*, 320.
9. Asahina, *Just Americans*, 75.
10. Ibid., 162.
11. Ibid., 192.
12. Inada, *Only What We Could Carry*, 284.

13. Daniels, *Prisoners Without Trial*, 79–80.

14. Robinson, *By Order of the President*, 224.

15. Asahina, *Just Americans*, 229.

16. Robinson, *By Order of the President*, 230.

17. Inada, *Only What We Could Carry*, 335–336.

18. Asahina, *Just Americans*, 230.

19. Robinson, *By Order of the President*, 231.

20. Asahina, *Just Americans*, 232.

CHAPTER 9

1. Daniels, *Prisoners Without Trial*, 89.

2. Ibid.

3. Ibid., 102.

4. Ibid., 105.

BIBLIOGRAPHY

Asahina, Robert. *Just Americans: How Japanese Americans Won a War at Home and Abroad: The Story of the 100th Battalion/442nd Regimental Combat Team in World War II*. New York: Gotham Books, 2006.

Berry, Henry. *"This Is No Drill!"—Living Memories of the Attack on Pearl Harbor*. New York: Berkley Publishing Group, 1992.

Daniels, Roger. *Prisoners Without Trial: Japanese Americans in World War II*. New York: Hill and Wang, 1993.

Inada, Lawson Fusao, ed. *Only What We Could Carry: The Japanese American Internment Experience*. Berkeley, Calif.: Heyday Books, 2000.

Irons, Peter. *Justice at War: The Story of the Japanese American Internment Cases*. Berkeley: University of California Press, 1983.

Japanese Eyes, American Heart: Personal Reflections of Hawaii's World War II Nisei Soldiers, compiled by the Hawaii Nikkei History Editorial Board. Honolulu: University of Hawaii Press, 2000.

Kashima, Tetsuden. Introduction to *Life Behind Barbed Wire: The World War II Internment Memoir of a Hawai'i Issei* by Yasutaro Soga. Honolulu: University of Hawaii Press, 2008.

Paterson, Thomas G., ed. *Major Problems in American Foreign Policy, Volume II: Since 1914*. New York: D.C. Heath and Company, 1989.

Robinson, Greg. *By Order of the President: FDR and the Internment of Japanese Americans*. Cambridge, Mass.: Harvard University Press, 2001.

Takaki, Ronald. *A Different Mirror: A History of Multicultural America.* Boston: Little, Brown and Company, 1993.

Takeuchi, Burt. "Pearl Harbor: Asian Americans Witness Air Raid on December 7th, 1941," online at http://us_asians.tripod.com/articles-nihonmachi-outreach.html, 12/02/2008.

FURTHER READING

BOOKS

Brimner, Larry Dane. *Voices from the Camps.* New York: Franklin Watts, 1994.

Fremon, David K. *Japanese-American Internment in American History.* Springfield, N.J.: Enslow Publishers, 1996.

Gordon, Linda and Gary Y. Okihiro, eds. *Impounded: Dorothea Lange and the Censored Images of Japanese American Internment.* New York: W.W. Norton and Company, 2006.

Gruenewald, Mary Matsuda. *Looking Like the Enemy: My Story of Imprisonment in the Japanese-American Internment Camps.* Troutdale, Ore.: New Sage Press, 2005.

McNaughton, James C. *Nisei Linguists: Japanese Americans in the Military Intelligence Service During World War II.* Washington, D.C.: Government Printing Office, 2006.

Ng, Wendy. *Japanese American Internment During World War II: A History and Reference Guide.* Westport, Conn.: Greenwood Press, 2002.

Tunnell, Michael O., and George W. Chilcoat. *The Children of Topaz: The Story of a Japanese-American Internment Camp; Based on a Classroom Diary.* New York: Holiday House, 1996.

WEB SITES
Densho: The Japanese-American Legacy Project

http://www.densho.org

This site has testimonies of Japanese Americans that were interned during World War II. Includes first-hand accounts, historical images, and teacher resources.

Discover Nikkei: Japanese American Military Experience Database

http://www.discovernikkei.org/en/resources/military/search/
?keywords=pacific&service_branch

This Web site is a resource for information about Japanese Americans. The site includes stories, photographs, video interviews, and articles in English and Japanese.

Go for Broke National Education Center

http://www.goforbroke.org

The Web site for the World War II Memorial Foundation was formed by the soldiers of the 100th Infantry Battalion, the 442nd Regimental Combat Team, and the Military Intelligence Service.

Japanese Internment (Documents), University of Illinois at Urbana-Champaign

http://www.library.uiuc.edu/doc/researchtools/guides/subject/
japaneseinternment.html

This Web site is an extension of the University of Illinois at Urbana-Champaign Government Documents Library exhibit on the internment of Japanese Americans. It is a starting point for research on the history and treatment of those that were interned during World War II.

PHOTO CREDITS

INDEX

ABOUT THE AUTHOR

JOHN C. DAVENPORT holds a Ph.D. from the University of Connecticut and currently teaches social studies at Corte Madera School in Portola Valley, California. Davenport is the author of several biographies and modern histories, including works on the American Revolution, the Japanese attack on Pearl Harbor, and the Nuremburg trials. He lives in San Carlos, California, with his wife, Jennifer, and his two sons, William and Andrew.